LOOK BACK AT OLD
BRYNMAWR

including
Beaufort, Clydach
& Llanelly Hill

by Malcolm Thomas

**Foreword by
PETER LAW J.P., A.M.**

Old Bakehouse Publications

Abertillery

First published in October 2004

ISBN 1 874538 23 9

Published in the U.K. by
Old Bakehouse Publications
Church Street,
Abertillery, Gwent NP13 1EA
Telephone: 01495 212600 Fax: 01495 216222
Email: oldbakehouseprint@btopenworld.com

Made and printed in the UK
by J.R. Davies (Printers) Ltd.

British Library Cataloguing in Publication Data: a catalogue
record for this book is available from the British Library.

Cynulliad National
Cenedlaethol Assembly for
Cymru Wales

Foreword

by Peter Law J.P., A.M.

As we look around us today it is easy to forget just how rich in industrial, social and cultural history our communities are. This is why I was delighted to be asked to write this foreword for Malcolm Thomas' new book, '*Look Back at Old Brynmawr, including Beaufort, Clydach and Llanelly Hill*'.

Within his book, Malcolm has done a great service to these communities by being able to revive wonderful memories of a by-gone age which I am sure will delight so many who will read this publication with major appreciation of the nostalgia that the photographs and their descriptions evoke.

Our proud communities were built on the contribution of so many of the people who are encapsulated forever within the chapters of this book and undoubtedly, it is a fitting tribute to the effort that so many made over so many years to establish these wonderfully warm communities which were built on traditional values and a belief in one's fellow human being. For many young people it will be a stark revelation just two years from the planned re-opening of the passenger rail service from Cardiff to Ebbw Vale to learn that Brynmawr once had its own very busy railway station, at the junction of which three main lines converged. And as always the centre piece for Brynmawr will always be our much loved Market Hall Cinema, which to this day provides strategic service in entertainment as the only cinema within the County Borough of Blaenau Gwent and surrounding areas.

Malcolm excels by producing this unique collection of photographs and captions that express to the world the great pride that has always been seen throughout our mining communities.

Today, at the beginning of our journey through the 21st Century, let us enjoy the content of this book, pausing for a moment and remembering what has been. Undoubtedly our communities will be enriched by this excellent publication.

Contents

FOREWORD

INTRODUCTION

                                                             Page

CHAPTER 1   BRYNMAWR TOWN   7

CHAPTER 2   LOCAL BUSINESSES AND COMMERCE   25

CHAPTER 3   TRANSPORT TO AND FROM THE TOWN   35

CHAPTER 4   LLANELLY HILL   41

CHAPTER 5   CLYDACH AND BLACK ROCK   63

CHAPTER 6   SOCIAL ACTIVITY AND EVENTS   75

CHAPTER 7   MATTERS OF RELIGION AND LEARNING   87

CHAPTER 8   BRYNMAWR THEN & NOW   101

CHAPTER 9   BEAUFORT   109

Introduction

My last book concerning a photographic history of Brynmawr and its neighbours was published in 1996, which I wrongly assumed would be the last such publication, given the amount of material thought to be available. Since then however, I have continued searching for, and collecting anything new and interesting, and consequently the result is this latest book, which at last, must be considered to be the finale! The two previous volumes also included chapters relating to Blaina and Nantyglo which on this occasion have been omitted, but are however, given their own identity in a new and completely separate book *'Look Back at Old Blaina and Nantyglo'*. In this will be seen a further interesting collection of some 200 photographs and illustrations portraying those districts.

So as the title of the book at hand suggests, Brynmawr, Beaufort, Clydach and Llanelly Hill are given as much attention as possible. The written history of the area has been recorded on a number of occasions, but with the added help of photographs, many people seem to agree that it becomes even more attractive, especially when one compares the scenes as they appear today, and what they looked like half a century or more ago. The region has been through some testing times over the years, the worst probably being the 1920s and '30s and alas, there are fewer and fewer people still with us now who can actually remember those days, hence the value of some of the photographs herein. Many migrated in search of better times and never returned, whilst those who stayed suffered the indignation of 'Means Tests' and charitable handouts. A publication by the Communist Party 'A Town on the Dole' summed up the situation all too well and whilst a number of once-important employers have deserted in recent years, things could never be as bad as they once were. Housing for instance was at a crisis level in the 1920s, with one report on Brynmawr revealing that of just over 1400 houses in the town, 180 of them were actually occupied by more than one family, not helped by only six new houses being built in a ten-year period and the local authority having to demolish a further 36 properties as being unfit for human habitation!

Just a mile or so away to the west is Beaufort, a town that was established in the year 1779 thanks to its pioneering ironmasters with such familiar names as Kendall and Bailey. There is a compilation of photographs that provide reminders of a typical Welsh valley town, with its ample supply of places of worship, public houses and a praiseworthy Male Voice Choir.

To the north of Brynmawr and facing each other across the valley are the villages of Clydach and Llanelly Hill, both of which are almost blessed with enough history and colourful characters to warrant a book in their own right. More mature readers who would have travelled from Brynmawr to Abergavenny on the bus down Black Rock could not have failed to notice 'Knight of the Road' - Jim Sharp and his self-imposed daily duty of directing the traffic through the narrow village. On the other side of the valley, where trains once ran, the services of 'Mrs Francis the Crossing' were called upon to control the railway crossing for a period of twenty-five years. On 'The Hill' itself, a complete list of characters would fill a page and include such names as 'Will the Van' who found that the serious courting of a certain fair lady was costing him far too much money so 'sold' her to his friend for two ounces of tobacco. Then there was Tom Williams 'Tommy the Miners' an unrestrained regular at the former Miners Arms pub, where it was said a night's consumption of 20 pints was common practice, his dying wish that his funeral cortege should pause for a moment outside the pub being granted. To add to the list would be Wally Yates the poacher, Nab Williams founder of the railway halt, Thomas Rees who delivered the milk until 90 years of age, William Jones long-time chronicler of the hills, and many should be grateful to Nurse Evans for their safe arrival on this earth, who as midwife, walked the length and breadth of the hillside in all weathers performing her duties. And so the list goes on.

In conclusion I hope therefore that within these pages will be found something to interest everyone.

Malcolm Thomas

CHAPTER 1

Brynmawr Town

1. In 1906 when this photograph was taken, Beaufort Street was overflowing with shops and traders, with more than sixty premises at the customers' call. To name but a few, there were 9 grocers, 7 butchers, and 4 each of drapers, shoe shops and confectioners. For those with a thirst, there were 9 public houses, Jones and Williams's Temperance Hotel and James Norwood's Refreshment Palace.

2. The most prominent building at the bottom of Beaufort Street has for very many years been The Griffin Hotel, seen here in 1906 and formerly known as The Castle before major reconstruction. During its heyday, this hotel was one of much eminence, attracting visiting businessmen and travellers, a delight being evening entertainment provided by local acclaimed harpist 'Will the Herring', so called it is said because of his rather emaciated appearance!

3. The development of Beaufort Street began as early as the 1830s with one or two shops and a few cottages to be seen. Those who were bold enough to contemplate starting a business of their own in those early days did not find it easy, thanks to the stranglehold held by the so-called 'Company Shops' and their wicked ways, that were operating at Clydach, Llanelly Hill, Nantyglo and Brynmawr itself by 1840. Even with the introduction of the Truck Act which outlawed 'payment in kind' and was supposed to do away with the ironmasters' hold over their workers' rights, it was well into the 1870s before Beaufort Street and the rest of the town could enjoy freedom of trade.

4. When this picture was taken at the bottom end of Beaufort Street in the mid 1930s, the serious economic depression that had dogged the town for almost ten years was at last beginning to lift. Between 1921 and 1931, Beaufort Street alone had lost 21 businesses to bankruptcy and failure and the press had by now dubbed Brynmawr as *'a dormitory town of 8,000 inhabitants, an official blackspot in a distressed area'.*

5. This is an exceptionally early photograph of the area that was to become the main square in Brynmawr, the scene pictured in about 1880 still showing evidence of the industrial tramroads that ran through the middle of the town. Precious limestone was brought from the quarries of Llangattock for onward shipment to the ironworks at Beaufort and Nantyglo.

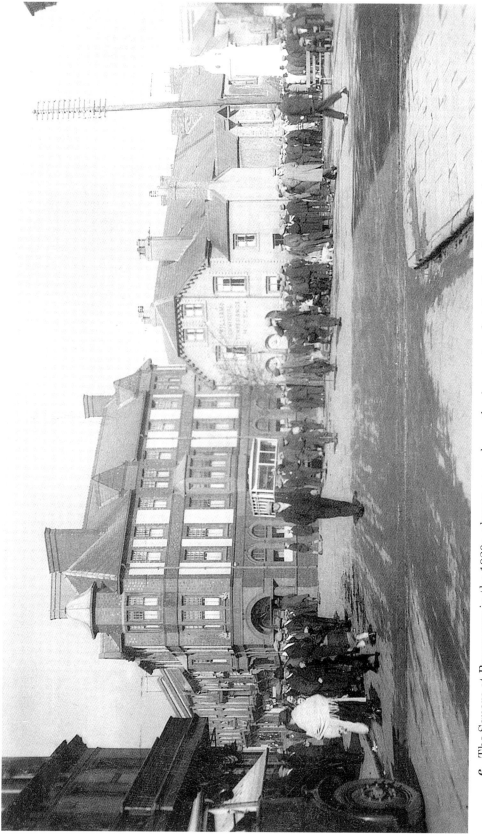

6. The Square at Brynmawr in the 1920s, always a popular gathering spot and at the time a bus arrival and departure point. A comprehensive bus service to and from the town commenced in 1922 with the formation of the Griffin Bus Company who opened their premises virtually where today's bus depot and garage is situated.

7. A crowd that is gathered around the War Memorial and a display of wreaths, suggest perhaps that this picture was taken shortly after an Armistice Day service. The largest crowd ever recorded to be present on the Square at one time was on Sunday 30th October 1927 when more than 3,000 gathered to admire the newly unveiled War Memorial.

8. A wintry view of the Market Hall in 1930. Up until the year 1800, Brynmawr was virtually uninhabited with just a scattering of farmhouses and cottages in the vicinity and the only traffic to be seen was on the road running from Abergavenny to Merthyr via the turnpike at nearby Clydach. In the early part of the nineteenth century, much was going on in the industrialised settlements of Clydach, Nantyglo and Beaufort with the consequent attraction of workers and their families to the area, thus creating a community in Brynmawr itself. A small number of shops, mostly operating from the parlours of private dwellings began trading to satisfy this gradually increasing population and the first Market Hall, with the intention of providing fresh produce and livestock for the town, was built in 1844 by popular demand. A number of alterations and extensions took place in subsequent years and although essentially a wholesale market (traders coming from as far as the north of England), a number of local shopkeepers also opened some stalls for business. Seeing an opportunity for further development, the local authority purchased the rights of the Market Company and a completely new and larger hall, as seen in this photograph, was built at public expense. The new building was opened on a day in 1894 with 200 specially selected guests invited to a 'spectacular luncheon and an event of pomp and circumstance'. The hall was now developed also as a place of entertainment featuring theatrical performances, concerts and dances and whilst seen by many as a great asset to the town, the stricter chapel-going fraternity condemned such activity as ungodly and made their voices heard far and wide. With the advent of moving pictures, a cinema was added in 1913, the building being leased to Dooner's Cinematograph Company at an agreed annual rent for periods of ten years at a time. Thus ninety years on it remains one of the few valley cinemas to have survived and a Saturday market has been held in Brynmawr for 150 years!

9./10. Brynmawr at an elevation of almost 400 metres above sea level is an easy target for any adverse weather conditions. The most disruptive years seem to have been 1947, 1963 and 1979 with newspaper headlines reading *'Town at a standstill'*, *'Four days without electricity'* and *'Helicopters dropping food and medical supplies'*. The upper photograph is of Somerset Street and below is Beaufort Street both seen during a long-running winter in April 1922 with men, shovels and a horse and cart to clear the highways.

11./12. Both of these views looking up and down Alma Street are from the 1950s and a much quieter thoroughfare than is to be found here today. On the left of the picture above is the former Wesleyan Chapel which had stood for a century before lack of support, in common with many other places of worship in the town, was closed and subsequently demolished. The name lives on however by way of 'Wesley House', a modern block of flats since erected on the site.

13./14. Two opposing views of the upper half of Alma Street showing the Library and Institute which was opened in 1906 with Mr. James Thomas the appointed librarian; the upper picture is from the 1950s and below, the period is the 1920s. Before the Institute was built, the town's first library and reading room was provided in the newly constructed Market Hall, the town council at the time anxious to be seen to be in compliance with the 1896 Public Libraries Act. A Council statement at the time read *'We must use all effectual means to secure this much needed means of education and character'*.

15. The featured building here is the Old Castle Inn, in days before it was demolished to make way for the New Griffin Hotel, its name taken from the older Griffin Hotel which stood on the corner at the top of Beaufort Street and King Street. The original Griffin was the headquarters of the town's stagecoach, Brynmawr being an important resting point on the coach road from Abergavenny to Merthyr Tydfil. Before the arrival of rail transport, the Griffin was the collection point for Brynmawr's mail, it being collected daily at 4pm by horsedrawn coach, whilst a special passenger service operated to Abergavenny on Tuesdays only.

16. King Street during the mid 1920s and a much less busy scene is to be witnessed. The main building on the left is the former Police Station, now of course converted into a private dwelling. Concerns about insurrection amongst disgruntled workers in the surrounding district led to the opening of the first Police Station in Brynmawr in 1849, with officer Thomas Jeremiah appointed in sole charge. When this photograph was taken however, the force had increased to include a superintendent, two sergeants and six constables with a Petty Sessional Court held on the premises every other Monday.

17. This elongated view of Orchard Street is somewhat different from the scene today, some fifty years later. Zoar chapel in the centre belonged to the Primitive Methodists or 'Ranters' to which they were often referred in early days. When demolished in the 1970s to make way for the present-day Community Centre, the extra-thick walls provided a few surprises, by revelation of a number of infant coffins which had been interred during the nineteenth century and of which no records appeared to be available; dignified re-burials were subsequently conducted in consecrated ground. The houses seen below the chapel are now a block of flats whilst most of the buildings on the opposite side of the road have been removed.

18./19. Two views of King Edward Road which are separated by some sixty years. The houses of King Edward Road, Intermediate Road and the lower half of Alma Street were constructed in the early 1900s - quality housing indicative of Brynmawr's growing prosperity. The large ornate house above once belonged to the Keysell family, proprietors of 'Saxons pop factory' which produced soft drinks from their works in Chapel Street for more than sixty years. The factory was demolished in the 1980s to make way for a housing block that is now appropriately named Saxon Court.

20. An additional view of King Edward Road in about 1922. Many of the town's houses built in the early 1900s were created by Building Societies, through which a number of residents of business and working classes invested their savings in house property. This boom was short-lived and with the intervention of World War One (1914-18), hardly any new development took place until the Urban District Council took over responsibility for house building from the Ministry and built their first 150 rental homes in the late 1920s.

21. Station Road in 1910 showing one of Brynmawr's largest shops of the era, James Richard Williams a dealer in all sorts of everyday wares. Part of the London and North Western Railway station is visible in the background as are a number of other shops open for business such as drapers, confectioners and Louis Powell the stonemason. The main store is now occupied by a supermarket.

22. The top end of Beaufort Street in 1922. A horse is being led up King Street and a police sergeant is seen passing the old Griffin Hotel. The Griffin was in its heyday a first-class hotel, affording 31 bedrooms and in great demand by commercial travellers in the district. In the background is the Board School, built in 1876 to replace the old British and Foreign School and capable of educating 1000 pupils of varying age when at its peak.

23. This penultimate photograph of the Square in this first chapter dates from 1937 and reveals further changes compared to the earlier views. Morgan's Temperance Hotel has been converted to the Café Royal and one of the town's first public telephone cubicles has appeared close by.

24. Greenland Road as it looked in about 1954. Housing here has been constructed in stages with the left-hand side being built in the early 1900s whilst those on the far right were some twenty years earlier and those on the near right appearing at the end of the 1920s. Even though this picture was taken in the 1950s, street lighting by gas (the town's first gasworks was built in 1849 in Chapel Street) was still in use judging by the lamp standards seen further along the road. Whilst electricity was widely available for industrial and commercial use for some twenty years previous, it was not adopted for lighting the streets of Brynmawr until 1934, even then at a most moderate pace.

25. The original photograph of this view describes it as 'The new road over the mountain to Waenavon'. Built shortly after the First World War, this road replaced what was just a rough track on the route to Blaenavon, then quite necessary upon the introduction of a regular bus service.

26. This final photograph in Chapter One must be one of the earliest-known, featuring the Market Square, and probably dates from the 1890's with John Morgan's Temperance Hotel offering an alcohol-free environment to its guests. The horse-drawn carriage is probably in the throes of conveying a paying guest to or from the railway station. With a careful eye looking beneath the window on the right, it may be possible to spot an interested dog posing for the photographer!

CHAPTER 2

Local Businesses and Commerce

27. The Capital and Counties Bank at No.72 King Street as pictured in 1910 when Mr. Sydney Padwick was the long-serving manager, also responsible for his sub branches at Blaina and Abercarn whilst additionally acting as treasurer to the U.D.C. During this period banks, along with most businesses had much longer working hours, they opening on Saturdays for instance from 9am until 2pm. The banking company was to become part of Lloyds in 1918 and re-named Lloyds TSB in 1995.

28. This 1950s view of the top of Beaufort Street may evoke a few memories after noticing the *'His Masters Voice'* sign hanging over the shop of Lyndon Sims, the record and radio dealer; he was also a well-known sports car enthusiast, competing at national and international levels. His other electrical shop was in Blaenavon whilst his father also ran a butcher's shop in King Street Brynmawr.

Gas Mantles, Globes, Fittings, &c.

of the very best quality,

can be obtained from

WEBB

115, Worcester Street, Brynmawr

(Next door to Post Office).

29. The period of this photograph would be the early 1920s when this particular shop belonged to Mr. Albert Matthews a general provisions dealer. Not recognisable today, it stood at No.48 Beaufort Street and the premises now form part of 'Alans Furnishers'.

30. Mr. Jonah Watkins and his wife are seen standing outside their fishmongers, fresh fruit and vegetable shop at No.16 Beaufort Street in 1901; the family also opened an additional shop in Station Road in later years. This former Beaufort Street shop was later to become 'Betty's Fashions' a familiar sight for many years and now adjacent to 'Records and Cards'.

31. The grocery store of William Pegler when it was situated at No.10 Beaufort Street, just below where today's Post Office stands. Pegler's first shop was much lower down the same street at No.29 which is now Rogers' shoe shop and finally in later years until closure in the 1970s, they had premises on the opposite side of the street next door to a competitor grocer namely Liptons.

32. Some readers may be excused for not recognising the whereabouts of this former Brynmawr public house, The Greyhound, as seen here in the early 1960s. The building is situated at No.13 Beaufort Street, on the corner with Worcester Street and nowadays will be better known as Rogers' Pet Store.

33. Another one-time popular pub was The Vulcan, situated on the corner of Bailey Street and King Street it was a nineteenth century inn and pictured here in about 1960. It has since been converted into a private dwelling although still easily recognisable thanks to the preservation of much of its original frontage.

34. The Royal Arms viewed shortly before its closure as licensed premises, used to stand on the corner of King Street and Queen Street. The adjacent houses, seen in the process of demolition, were replaced by newer properties whilst the pub building itself was retained and subsequently converted into a private house, namely No.66 King Street.

35. Yet another nineteenth-century public house no longer in existence is the Fireman's Arms at No.19 Worcester Street. Demolition work is seen in progress on the corner with Somerset Street, with a number of buildings being pulled down to allow the construction of a new Police Station. The pile of rubble is now a residents' car park and the 'Fireman's' has been converted into a block of flats aptly named Fireman's Court.

ROYAL EXCHANGE

36. Nearing the end of a collection of photographs of Brynmawr's public houses in this chapter is this montage featuring the Royal Exchange with Freda Morgan in charge in Davies Street which is still open for custom, one of just a dozen remaining in the town. A hundred years ago there were around 40 pubs and at least another 12 beer retailers available, hence the need maybe for the various temperance movements that found popular support at the time. Such was the concern of many, that local souls were being lost to the evil drink, a branch of the British Women's Temperance Association was established in Alma Street in about 1908 with Miss Susan Thomas as its loyal secretary for many years.

"LADY R." The Guideless Wonder,
The Property of Mr. THOS. BAYTON, Newcastle Stores, Beaufort Street, Brynmaur, South Wales.

37. This is a business advertisement card issued by Thomas Bayton in 1910 promoting the services of his stores and inn, The New Castle which stood at the bottom of Beaufort Street. These premises now belong to a popular bread and cake shop.

38. Possibly one of the most memorable landmarks in Brynmawr's history was the Semtex factory with its 'state of the art' domed roof. Officially opened for production in 1951 at a cost of just over a million pounds, it provided valuable jobs for some 30 years, and the site was a topic of discussion and protest for more than 20 years before final demolition took place.

39. An inspection team consisting of C. Watkins and Selwyn Ford at the end of a floor-tile production line at Dunlop Semtex. Ideas for building the factory started as early as 1945, promoted by Lord 'Jim' Forrester who had spent so much effort in association with the Quakers in lifting Brynmawr out of its economic gloom in the early 1930s. After his elevation to Managing Director of Enfield Cables Ltd. he had a post-war yearning to return to the town and continue his work by creating up to 1,000 jobs in a new subsidiary factory he had in mind. Opened in July 1951, it was to be known as The Brynmawr Rubber Company, producing a wide range of rubber merchandise including shoe soles and floor tiles. Fortunes were short-lived however, and the operation ran into serious financial difficulties within a year, forcing a hurried closure. It was almost two years before the Dunlop Company was persuaded to consider the site as a production base and once agreed, this was seen as the new beginning. So it was, and by 1959 the factory space was increased to more than 300,000 square feet with production concentrating on the new plastic floor tiles that were rapidly replacing the traditional floor-coverings. Dunlop was soon one of the world's largest manufacturers of vinyl tile products and confidently invested a further £5 million in the Brynmawr factory in 1964. To further enhance their standing as a modern-thinking employer, with employee welfare in mind the company purchased the old Brynmawr Bootmakers factory in Pond Road and opened a popular social club there. Sadly recession and overseas competition began to bite in the early 1970s and a series of redundancies and strikes by an angry workforce spelled doom. Matters came to a head in the winter of 1981 with a factory 'sit-in' that lasted through the Christmas period, culminating with the announcement of total closure in January 1982 and that was the end - well not quite! The site was to remain a derelict eyesore for another 19 years before decisions and agreements were finally reached as to how to proceed. The subject of so much argument and protest in the end turned out to be the fate of the domed roofs and whether they could be considered for 'listed building status'. A 'Brynmawr Rubber Factory Action Group' was formed with the aim of preserving what they saw as a vital piece of the town's industrial history and gathered protests, attracting much media attention were organised outside the factory gates. Despite all this however, the authorities eventually won the day and on June 25th 2001 contractors moved in and ended an era. Development plans with a cost of millions of pounds, are now afoot to transform the whole area creating housing and shopping facilities that will make this part of Brynmawr hardly recognisable without the help of comparative photographs.

40. The lower end of Beaufort Street in about 1920 and the shops on the right-hand of the street include Alf Watkins the butchers (the premises now a newsagents) who also farmed at the Old Bryn Farm. Next door is Mr. Thomas James's grocery shop, adjacent to a tobacconists and followed by one of three shops owned by Mr. William Howell who dealt in confectionery, outfitting and drapery.

41. Garlands and decorations adorn what is believed to be the Old Castle Hotel at the bottom of Beaufort Street in the early 1900s. In a window can be seen mention of ales and stout Rhymney, which would have referred to Andrew Buchan's Rhymney Brewery which had been supplying beers to the valleys since 1838. The famous 'Hobby Horse' trademark was to be seen decorating many of Brynmawr's drinking establishments.

42. In these days of the many social benefits that are available to the sick and unemployed through state funding, it is hard to imagine an existence without it. Life in Brynmawr in the early 1930s however meant 'existence' and nothing more, for it was christened 'A town on the dole'. Unemployment throughout South Wales had been consistently high for more than ten years, reaching 33% in 1931, Brynmawr however more than doubled that and 'Something must be done' became the catchphrase. To make matters worse, in October 1931, an already meagre unemployment benefit was cut by 20% and 'The Means Test' was introduced, supposedly to test a family's assets against their actual needs and level of benefit payable (it was later reported that this exercise had been a complete waste of time in Brynmawr as most families' possessions consisted of no more than what they stood up in!). Another devastating blow at the same time was the withdrawal of two free school meals a day for the neediest of children, to be substituted by free milk only thus putting further pressure on the weekly housekeeping budget. In despair of perceived government ignorance of the town's plight, the local community took it upon themselves to put matters right. In April 1931 a committee was formed consisting of members from a number of organisations including the Brynmawr Community Study Council and various Christian Movements who began to organise a Voluntary Service Camp to be set up in the town throughout the summer. Some 70 volunteers from numerous professions beckoned to the call coming from the United Kingdom, Europe and even the U.S.A. all offering their services. Men were billeted in some totally unfurnished rooms above unused shops with a few rough shelves and straw mattresses and makeshift beds. The female volunteers fared better in another disused building with some beds on loan from some of the locals. The task at hand was to assist some of the town's unemployed in transforming a large rubbish dump and tip from an unhealthy eyesore into a recreation park that will be seen in a further chapter. The photograph here is of some lady-volunteers who prepared food and washing facilities for the workers in a tin hut on the site which also served as their canteen.

CHAPTER 3

Transport to and from the Town

43. The precise date here is Wednesday July 12th 1905 and celebrations are in progress at Brynmawr station as the first train is about to depart for Nantyglo on the newly opened 2 miles of railway line. Ever since the opening of the Brecon and Merthyr line in 1862 linking the town with Abergavenny and a few years later in 1869, when the London and North Western Railway opened up their route to Blaenavon, questions were asked why the western valley line from Newport should suddenly terminate at Nantyglo. This was seen as a great inconvenience particularly by the traders of the town who raised their first major protest in 1877. At the time, local shopkeepers did much of their wholesale trade with the merchants of Bristol who shipped their goods to Newport for further handling by The Monmouthshire Railway and Canal Company. An important meeting was held at Bristol with a view to re-directing goods to Cardiff thus depriving the Monmouthshire Company of vital business, but even this threat fell on deaf ears. Arguments on all sides prevailed for years thereafter, the railway company on economic grounds and the traders and travelling public claiming that additional travelling facilities would, without fail, bring shoppers to the town rather than attract them from it. Nevertheless, another 28 years passed before the matter was finally settled.

Brynmawr · "Missing Link" Railway.

THE FIRST TRAIN WILL BE SIGNALLED BY

HER GRACE THE DUCHESS OF BEAUFORT

TO RUN AT 1.35 P.M.

On Wednesday Next, July 12th, 1905.

RETURN FARE   -   3D.

44. The last scheduled passenger train to travel from Abergavenny through Brynmawr was on a cold Sunday, January 5th 1958 and is pictured here at Brynmawr station, the next stop being Beaufort and a last visit to the already defunct Ebbw Vale High Level. Hauled by two steam locos, the leading engine which was built in 1888, was driven by Mr. George Lewis with the assistance of Derek Hinton. Providing a booster was the much more modern locomotive in the hands of another pair of highly-experienced railwaymen Mr. F. Brown and Mr. A. Baker.

45. The love of steam trains is open to all ages and does not fade as evidenced by the enthusiasts photographed with a Stephenson Locomotive Society Special at Brynmawr facing in the direction of Blaenavon in May 1962.

46. The year is approximately 1957 but the time of the train's arrival is more precise, at 12.21pm having just journeyed from Newport. It is standing at the timber-made platform (with no shelter incidentally), constructed to serve the western valley traffic once the link with Nantyglo had been completed in 1905.

47. Passenger services on the mountainous line between Brynmawr and Blaenavon came to an end through lack of custom (there being about four trains a day through to Newport) in 1941. Then came 'the Dr. Beeching era' and all passenger traffic in the western valley was withdrawn in April 1962, albeit goods services operated for a few years more.

48. Looking towards the town with the familiar landmark of the Semtex power house in view, the scene is a sad one as the station is seen in the process of dismantling in the 1960s. In its day Brynmawr was quite a busy station and for many years before the Second World War travel by train was most attractive. Special 'Market Day' fares were introduced for trips to the town on Saturdays and special inclusive train and admission tickets were available to Abertillery with its numerous cinemas.

49. A final look from one of the station's platforms when the signals and signal box were still intact. The line bearing to the left went on to Clydach and all stations to Abergavenny (see Chapter Five), whilst straight on and under the bridge was the long mountainside curve up to Waunavon and on to Blaenavon High Level. All of the area seen here has been superseded by roads and roundabout whilst the hill leading to Waunavon can be seen in the background.

50. Although closed to passenger traffic in May 1941, this 'Special', hauled by a Pannier Tank loco is stood at the platform of the elevated station at Waunavon 1957. The lines between Blaenavon and Brynmawr remained open for another 25 years or so transporting coal within the area, as Waunavon was well-worked as an opencast coal site. The only evidence remaining of this station is the former station house, now converted into a private dwelling.

51. An early petrol-engined omnibus as it was more commonly known when this picture was taken on the Market Square in 1927. The bus belongs to the Griffin Company who started their business in Brynmawr in 1921 at the old Griffin yard (where today's bus garage stands), hence the adoption of the company name. The bus in question, which would have been in the company's red and cream livery, was one of two 'brand new' 'Dennis' 1½ton 20 seaters bought in October 1926 to add to their growing fleet and was the showpiece on all the company's documents and advertisements. For a number of years it was used as a one-man operated bus on the Crickhowell service, but the pull placed on its relatively small engine up the Black Rock must have proved too much, for the vehicle was dispensed with in 1930 - four years being a rather curtailed career for a bus!

52. On the square in 1950 waits a Griffin bus ready for the journey to Blackwood via Crumlin and the vehicle is a diesel-engined Leyland Tiger which came off the production line in Lancashire in May 1937. Not having a local number plate, it is probably an ex-demonstration model which would have been sold off by the manufacturer when no longer needed. Griffin paid £1382 for this model and is seen here in its original livery, it later ending up in the hands of the Red and White Company.

53. This concluding photograph was also taken in 1950 outside 'Marie's Café' which was a favourite place for refreshment for bus staff and passengers. The bus, is a 'Ralph's' (who later formed a 'holding company' Griffin-Ralph Ltd. in conjunction with Red and White Services), manufactured by Albion-Duple, a model that many drivers claimed was far too underpowered for the hills around Brynmawr.

CHAPTER 4

Llanelly Hill

54. One of Llanelly Hill's surviving landmarks is the 'Jolly Colliers' and it is pictured here in 1906 when Mr. Alexander McIntyre was the landlord. Taking into account the three neighbouring hamlets of Llanelly Hill, Clydach and Black Rock there were sixteen public houses and three independent beer retailers serving the community at the turn of the 19th and 20th centuries. By providence however there were at least eight places of worship within easy reach, attracting a far larger following.

55. The same public house is now seen some fifty years later with long-serving landlord Mr. Gwilym Powell stood outside, he being the locally trained village cobbler under the watchful eye of Mr. Button before moving into the licensed trade. The pub owners, the Rhymney Brewery and presumably the local health authority, for quite a number of years allowed one of the rooms to be used (not during licensing hours incidentally) as the village surgery with visiting GPs Jack and Merlyn Farrington holding weekly consultations; the practice was later transferred to more subtle surroundings in the village hall.

56. Taking a 'breather' outside The Jolly Colliers during the 1950s are a few of the 'regulars' and amongst the group are Horace Walker, Walter Yates, Dennis Paynter, Jack Waters, Des Waters, Freddie Parry, Matt Williams, Tilly Jones and Gwillym Powell. Horace may be well-remembered being seen walking on the hill despite the fact that he only had one leg, but, as more than one local remarked in the nicest possible way, his vocal talents inside the pub left much to be desired!

57. A wide-angled view of The Hill from the 1950s with the houses of The Gelli in the foreground. At the top of the picture are a few familiar buildings, some of which are no longer there - Miles' Row, Beersheeba Chapel and Ysgol Ddu. A little further down, below the railway bridge seen on the left of the picture is Cwm Paca (Valley of the Goblin) site of 'Shakespeare's Cave' where legend has it the great bard once paid a visit and conceived his work 'A Mid-summer Night's Dream'.

58. Another group of local customers outside The Jolly Colliers some fifty years ago includes Gwillym Powell, Walter Yates, John Walby and Ivor Symonds. Walter was said to have been a dedicated 'herbalist', claiming to never have caught a cold and would regularly be seen 'humping' coal and the like around the village despite being severely handicapped, his skills as the local poacher were also appreciated by many.

59. A crowd of villagers pictured outside their holiday hotel probably at Blackpool in the 1950s and amongst the familiar faces are Gwyn Williams, Ike Jones, Malcolm Rees, Byron Jones, Mary Jones, Clarice Jones, Trevor Jones, Lou Jones, Mrs. Williams, Cyril Francis, Glyn Davies, Mrs. Rogers and son, Delwyn Simmonds, Jack Waters, Lily Mizen, Maggie Roberts, David McCloy, Evelyn Francis, Carl James, Doris Mills, Mrs. Waters, Jimmy Roberts, Norma Simmonds, Sheila Jenkins, Annie Baldwin, Teresa Lole, Mag Lloyd, Jack Lloyd, Lily Mills and Doris Mills.

60. Workers at 'Pinchie Colliery' in about 1890 (the gentleman in the bowler hat being the traditionally-dressed gaffer), which was one of a number of privately owned coal-levels on Llanelly Hill. This level at the top of the hill near Waunavon, employed 250 men in its heyday and was owned by the Williams brothers of Brynmawr with Noah Lewis as manager. The Black Vein coal seam actually passed under Wood House which is still there, but the colliery owners were obliged to make a slight detour after the then owners of the house protested their worries of subsidence. Pinchie colliery eventually closed in the mid-1940s after most of the seam was worked out and the Williams brothers went into retirement.

61. Local inhabitants and probably the current owners of this property will not easily recognise what was a farmhouse pictured here some 80 or 90 years ago. For this is 'Field House' and posing for the photographer is Sarah-Jane (Granny) Jones. In the depression years of the 1930s, a report on the area claimed that the hamlet of Llanelly Hill was a far more prosperous place to live than Brynmawr thanks to its number of wise hillside collier-farmers, men whose subsidiary occupation of agriculture helped see them through the most difficult of times of the mining industry.

62. A large gathering of local children dominates the interior of the Welfare Hall probably dressed for a stage performance in the 1930s. Voluntary effort by the mining fraternity in providing a wide variety of social interests for the community should never be underestimated typically demonstrated with the building of Llanelly Hill's Hall in 1933 with President of The South Wales Mining Federation and Member of Parliament Arthur Jenkins performing the opening ceremony. The gentleman on the far left of this photograph is Mr. James Davies who for a number of years was chairman of the trustees of the hall.

63. Soccer has been a mainstay of sport on Llanelly Hill for more years than most can remember and here is the victorious team of 1956 after winning the Abertillery League. In the black and white stripes from left to right are - Back: Ainsley Morgan, Colin Lewis, Joe Thomas, Brian Watkins (Beaufort), Dennis Dullea and Howard Emery. Front: Clive Morgan, Eric Walby, Lawrence Bosley, John McCloy and Len Cox.

64. A significant photograph taken of the ladies at the Wesleyan chapel on August 3rd 1953 following the ceremony of the first wedding to be solemnised there. The 'helping hands' are Maggie (Claud) Roberts, Maggie (Fanna) Roberts, Mrs. Coleman (Lodge), Kate Evans, Mrs. Clare, Mrs. Jones, Mrs. Prosser, Mrs. Francis, Mrs. Welch and Mrs. Bristow.

65. This picture records a village outing to Rhossili on the Gower coast in the summer of 1956 with Rees's coaches at hand. The trippers include Mr. and Mrs. Edmund Williams, Mr. and Mrs. Israel Paynter, Mr. and Mrs. Ivor Jones, Mr. and Mrs. Johnny Bishop, Mr. and Mrs. Tom Coleman, Mr. and Mrs. Alf Silman, Mr. and Mrs. Collett, Mr. and Mrs. Donald Lewis, Mr. and Mrs. Bert Puddle, Clarice Jones, Evelyn Davies, Sheila Jones, Margo Rees, Miss Coleman and Tom Jones (Cow).

66. Darenfelin School in the 1960s and most of the names have been provided, with apologies to the unknowns, reading left to right. Back: Mrs. White, Susan Munster, David Yates, Susan Davies, Glyn Sherman, Stephen Baldwin, Valerie Roberts, Mrs. Mann. 2nd Row: Michele Lewis, Kay Marshall, Malcolm Collett, Dale Walters, Julie Michael, Lynne Williams. 3rd Row: Keri Owens, Andrew McCloy, Trevor Gwillym. Front?, Mandy Jones.

67. Some more pupils in the same classroom as above to include the following- Back: Catherine Reames, Christine Welch, Jeff Cunvin, Judith Baldwin, Mrs. Mann, Leslie Evans, John Shephard, Mark Williams, Joy Gwillym. Middle: David Reames, Paul Edwards, Mark Jones, Karen Parton, Susan Jones, Maureen Archibald, Jane Hill. Front: Gwyn Williams, Chris Aylett, Caroline McCloy, Carol Michael, Meirion Williams.

68./69. No village should be without its annual carnival event as proved by these two photographs taken during the 1950s. Above the well-decorated lorry is passing the 'Colliers' with Margaret Bates as the carnival queen ably assisted by Norma Symonds and Pauline Rogers. Below is another 1950s event with Maureen Walters' turn as queen but unfortunately only one court lady has been identified, that being Glynis Walters.

70. This time it's the Hill's gentlemen to have 'star' roles in the carnival with Emrys (Dick Williams) as the Zulu warrior. The onlooker in the 1950s trilby hat is Emlyn Powell.

Llanelly Hill Hearse & Burial Fund.
(*Established 1929*)

✂️⁂

RULES

Governing all Collectors and Committeemen.

71. These local footballers are pictured on the Recreation Ground in about 1950 and left to right they are Graham Rees, Melvyn Jones, Owen Powell (his back to the camera unfortunately), Des Waters and Carson Thomas. The land for the grounds was originally given to the village by local farmer and J.P. Mr. Seth Puddle and work in preparing it was started during the 1926 General Strike. The mining fraternity was well-known for its welfare interests until the break-up of the industry, with weekly contributions of as little as 1p per week funding a number of institutions. Out of this Llanelly Hill's War Memorial and Welfare Hall was opened in 1933.

72. The last remaining place of worship in the area is Mount Zion Methodist which has served its followers since the year 1860. Regular Sunday services are held in the evenings during the summer months and afternoons during the winter and to quote a member *'the only reserved seat is the organist's - all are welcome'*.

73. Besides Mount Zion there were once four other religious establishments to choose from, Beersheeba Baptist, Calvinistic Methodist, Bethel Congregational and the Mission Room. The Mission room was originally the Clydach Company Shop which after closure, was gifted to the vicar of Llanelly who after raising some £200, converted it into a place of worship. Mount Zion or the Wesleyan to which it is better known has, over the years seen a number of improvements and alterations and whilst the original building was erected in 1860, the chancel and school-room were added later. Up until 1951 heating and lighting were provided by a coal fire and paraffin lamps then to everyone's delight, electricity was introduced to the village and although almost a century old, it was not until 1953 that the chapel was licensed for marriages.

74. The weekend of July 3rd and 4th July 1993 was a most important period in Zion's long history, celebrating the completion of vital restoration work. For some time the church's future was in grave doubt until the parishioners stood together and launched a campaign that realised the raising of £20,000 to preserve what was not only a place of worship, but a village landmark. The guest of honour was the late orator and politician Viscount Tonypandy, who is seen here with Janet Preece, Pauline Rogers, Irene Roberts, Jocelyn Owen and Claire Rogers.

75. The restoration work, amongst much else, included replacing ancient pews with new chairs but the old timber did not go entirely to waste. Local craftsman Douglas Rees used some of it to produce Welsh love spoons which were sold to augment the funds. Viscount Tonypandy is seen here in discussion with Mr. Rod Ingrouville who was Minister at the time, having led the service of thanksgiving and rededication to a mass congregation on the Sunday.

76. A school photograph from 1958 with headmaster Mr. Bill Roberts on the right and teacher Mrs.V. Harrington on the left. The pupils pictured left to right are Back: A. Price, E. Quebell, B. Tinkler, R. Vaughan, L. Davies, unknown, J. Gravell, R. Davies. Middle: M. Thomas, V. Howard, C. Brooks, J. Coleman, G. Lewis. Front: S. Alexander, E. Rudge, unknown, C. Davies, R. Roberts, J. Walters, J. Roberts, C. Williams.

77. The date is July 1974 with a photograph taken to mark the retirement of Mrs. Margaretta Puddle who has just been presented with a clock by headmaster Mr. Ford on behalf of the pupils, staff and friends. Mrs. Puddle who originally joined the kitchen staff as a 'helper', went on to be appointed in charge, providing much-appreciated school dinners for an astounding 30 years!

78. The teaching staff at the school in 1924 at a time when it was capable of managing the education of 300 pupils. Some of the names traced are Miss S.J. Coleman and Miss E.A. Rosser (seated 2nd and 3rd from the left), Mr. S. Pearce (Headmaster) with Mr. D. Jenkins far right. Behind Mr. Jenkins is Miss M. Fanner, later to become Mrs. M. Roberts (Waunavon); Miss Fanner's family for a number years kept the Jolly Colliers and the school that is left today caters for just 35 pupils up to the age of 11.

79. Some of the Under 16s players at Bailey Park in about 1950 with Llanelly Hill beating Abergavenny 2-1 in the final. The youngsters include Nobby Jones, Ron Bevan, Clive Morgan, Eric Walby, Lawrence Bosley, Warren Kershaw and John McCloy.

80. Gelly United AFC during the 1933-34 season and in the picture left to right are: Back: E. Roberts, E. Edwards, P. Williams. Middle: E. Edwards (Treasurer), W. Jones, K. Hall, J. Meale, T. Davies (Chairman), J.C. Davies (Secretary). Front: D. Walters, A. Davies, C. Thomas (Capt.), H. Roberts, W. Thomas.

81. Beersheeba Chapel closed in the 1980s but not before these Sunday School pupils could be photographed with the Junior School in the background. Where possible, names given include - Back: Heather Gwillym (holding baby brother Nigel), Michelle Lewis, Vanessa Rees, Mandy Jones, Mark Jones, Debbie Poyner, ?, ?. Front and middle: Ms. Warfield, Mandy Williams, ?, Ms. Gwillym, Mstr. Gwillym, Donna Poyner, Ms. Warfield, John Jones, Margaret Jones, ?, ?.

82. Beersheeba Sunday School Anniversary is celebrated in this 1969 photograph. Just in front of the children was the 'open-air' baptismal pool and on record is the baptism of a group of children in December 1955, when head deacon Dan Gunter ingeniously and with good intent ran back and forth from the chapel with kettles of hot water trying to comfort the very disgruntled babes - this arrangement was not to be repeated however! Some names in this picture are Deborah Gwillym, Caroline McCloy, Debbie Poyner, Vanessa Rees, Mandy Jones, Maxine and Marilyn Lewis, Michelle Lewis, Andrew McCloy, Nigel Rees, Diane Poyner, Donna Poyner, Margaret Jones, Mr. Gwillym, Mandy Williams, Ms. Gwillym, Paula Jones.

83. The ladies of Beersheba Chapel Sisterhood who are posed for this photograph probably during the 1950s are as follows - Rachel Jones, Dulcie Bishop, Gert Gunter, Melver Gunter, Sally Jones and Alicia Curran.

84. Beersheeba Chapel as it appeared on opening in 1836 before the addition of a vestry to the left of the building. Ancient records show that during the great cholera outbreak of 1849, the minister at the time Mr. Thomas Griffiths had recruited a regular Sunday night congregation of 250 souls who sought spiritual comfort and deliverance from the dreaded disease but much to his dismay, saw it fall to an average of just 90 once the scare had subsided and their prayers had been answered. Unfortunately however, the once-loved Rev. Griffiths' esteem suddenly fell into disrepute in 1882, necessitating a mysterious and hurried emigration to America! This though was just an isolated incident in the chapel's 150-year existence, the site now being occupied by a private dwelling.

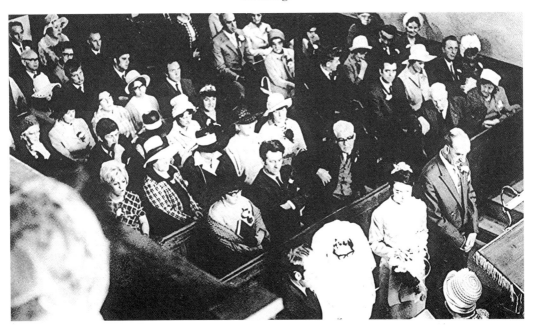

85. An interior view of Beersheeba in the 1970s with the wedding of Stella Lewis and Gerald Sherman being officiated by lay-preacher Freda Jones. Born and bred on 'The Hill', Freda, a retired nurse, is still to be found conducting services in the Abergavenny area. Many ministers served the chapel over the years and a few names that might be remembered include Mr. Bishop, Ron Davies, Don Harding, Mr. Stephens, Vera Withers, Tommy Gwillim and Doug Davies of Clydach.

86. Darenfelen as it looked in 1920 with some buildings yet to appear ten years later the distance such as the Welfare Hall and Infants' School. Although not seen here, brief mention must be made of Gelli-Felen and its unique little railway halt which was to make its first appearance in 1933. Championed by Mr. Naboth Williams, local residents petitioned the London, Midland and Scottish Railway Company for years to have their own station at Llanelly Hill arguing that there was good passenger business to be had with villagers travelling in either direction to Brynmawr or Abergavenny. The company finally conceded to the demand and a halt was constructed and officially opened with lavish celebrations on Wednesday September 6th 1933. The importance that the inhabitants placed on what might seem a trivial event by today's standards, may be appreciated by reading some of the following extracts from the order of ceremony -

A Special Train will leave Brynmawr at 2.45 pm to convey all invited by card (from Mr. Naboth Williams).

The Rector of Llanelly Parish Rev. Gurnos Davies and Clerk to the Council. Mr. W.H. Powell J.P. will extend, on behalf of the inhabitants of the area, a welcome to visitors.

The tape across the entrance gate on the Gelli-Felen side of the railway line will then be cut by His Worship The Mayor of Abergavenny, with a scissors presented to him by Mrs. Margaret Walters, the oldest lady residing at Gelli-Felen.

The tape across the gate at the bottom of the new footpath will be cut by His Worship The Mayor of Brecon, with a scissors presented to him by Mrs. Mary Ann Bevan, oldest lady of Cwmnantgam.

The tape across the gate at the top of the new path will be cut by Mrs. C.H. Tait, with a scissors presented to her by Mrs. Martha Brooks, oldest lady of Upper Gelli.

The children of the Gelli-Felen area will then be invited to take a free trip on the train to Brynmawr and back.

All guests will then form a procession at the top of the new path, led by Blaina Town Band to Darenfelen School where a tea will be provided for ticket holders at 1/6d (7¹/₂p) per person. A ham sandwich tea will be available for children under the age of 14 for 6d (2¹/₂p).

And so the celebrations, almost as grand as the opening of the major stations at Brynmawr and Abergavenny, continued into the evening with a crowded public meeting at Carmel Methodist Chapel addressed by a string of dignitaries and railway company officials culminating in a rapturous rendering of 'Guide Me O Thy Great Jehova' to the tune of Cwm Rhondda. Inevitably, what was to become known as 'Nab Halt', the railway and Nab Williams himself are now just another piece of local history.

87. Pictures from the 1950s when it was possible to take a train from Abergavenny onwards, at the same time enjoying the delightful scenery of the Clydach valley. The concept of constructing a railway communication between Abergavenny and Merthyr Tydfil was first debated in the mid-1850s, the period of a thriving iron industry across the heads of the valleys. A company bearing the title of 'The Merthyr, Tredegar and Abergavenny Railway Co.' was formed under the chairmanship of entrepreneur and M.P. Crawshay Bailey, with members of the public and commerce being invited to purchase shares in an exciting new venture at £20 a share. All of this activity actually proceeded on the assumption that the government of the day would authorise such a project in the first place; fortunately for the investors, an Act was passed without hitch on August 1st 1859. Work however did not begin until June 1860 with Mrs. Crawshay Bailey cutting the first sod on a patch of grassland at Abergavenny, which was to become the site of Brecon Road station and nowadays a doctors' surgery. Despite serious concerns regarding the steep gradient through Clydach gorge, tunnelling and viaduct building, the task was finally completed and the first train from Abergavenny to Brynmawr ran on September 29th 1862, followed by four trains per day in each direction. Travel from Brynmawr onwards across the heads of the valleys was conducted by a once-daily horse-drawn coach before the line was extended, it being 1864 before it reached Nantybwch for a connection with Tredegar. Conveniently close to Clydach station for some were two licensed premises, the New Clydach Inn and the Railway Inn (now a private dwelling) and nearby, Nazareth Chapel, now also converted into a private house. Tribute must be paid to Mrs. Evelyn Francis who had the important duty of controlling the railway crossing at Clydach for 25 years, she being the third generation of the same family that had been doing the job since the station opened. Mrs. Francis lived in one of two adjoining cottages nearby, and those wishing to use the crossing would ring the gate bell whence she would allow them through having carefully checked that all was clear. Inevitably she was to be known just as 'Mrs. Francis the Crossing' and some locals may still remember her next door neighbour Dan Gunter, the local council worker. Upon Mrs. Francis's retirement after the line closed in January 1958, she had earned herself a grand retirement pension of £1 per week!

88. An ensemble of young stars pictured after the performance of the annual Nativity play at Darenfelin School in the late 1950s and most of their names have been retrieved as follows with apologies for possible errors and omissions - Back: (left to right) Jeanette Emery, Moira Preece, Marilyn Lewis, John Murphy, Deryn Croucher, Michael Thomas, Glenn Lewis, Robert Lewis, Gwenfron Powell, Virginia Howard, Lyn Davies, Janette Coleman, Nadina Davies, Maxine Lewis, David Evans, Barbara Allen, Shaun Alexander; ?; Donald Griffiths, Lynne Rogers. Kneeling: Angela Bosley, Linda Edwards, Veronica Murphy, Jane Price, ?; Sharon Simmonds, Gethin Watts, David Cox, Susan Davies, Janet James, ?, Anita Price, Susan Price, Robin Williams, David Archibald, Robert Davies.

89. Staff and pupils are seen in the yard of the newly-opened Darenfelen Council Infants' School. This school catering for the youngest of pupils was officially opened on Saturday January 31st 1931 but prior to this, pupils of mixed ages attended the older building on the opposite side of the road. However the government-sponsored Hadow Report of 1930 called for major national re-classification and segregation of junior education into three groups namely infants (under 7 years), juniors (7 to 11) and seniors (11 and above) hence one of the reasons for opening Darenfelen which served its pupils for fifty years before closure.

90./91. This chapter of the book would not be complete without mention of the Rees family, members of which have occupied the Hill for a century and more. Here are two, out of a total of four sons and four daughters, the offspring of Albert and Barbara Rees with Doug (left) and brother Thomas (right). Doug will be remembered as a master of Welsh Love Spoon carving, samples of which have found their way as far afield as the U.S.A. and Canada and thankfully the ancient craft has been passed on to his son Martin. Thomas of course was better known as Thomas The Milk who delivered the beverage until he reached an incredible 90 years of age, armed with a photographic memory of every one of his customers requirements without ever having to consult his list.

92. On the left is the familiar face of Bert Rees, a patriarch of transport in the district. He began his business on leaving school in 1923 with the purchase of a horse and cart, used for delivering bread before his first motorised acquisition, a six-seater Overland open-top car. Next came his first lorry which saw a novel usage including the addition of wooden benches for the transportation of miners to big Pit at Blaenavon and when that was done, out came the seating to make way for the collection of the 'ashes' from Llanelly Hill, Clydach and even Crickhowell. Another important contract was the delivery of fresh water from a tank that had to be filled from a tap in Gilwern; this being a common problem at the time, there being insufficient pressure to serve those who were lucky enough to possess a tap in Llanelly Hill. This first lorry of the Rees Company also had one further occasional use, that of the local hearse! By the late 1920s, Bert bought his first bus, a 14-seater Chevrolet which was probably a leftover from the First World War, and so started a regular passenger service to Brynmawr and Abergavenny market, a service that continues to this day. Steady progress was made with the business and just after the Second World War two new coaches were purchased at £700 each. Nevertheless, these were austere days and actual passenger comfort was not a priority as far as the bus manufacturers were concerned. The choice of colour was limited to brown and nothing else, fitted out with 29 wooden-slatted seats for which passengers wisely took their own cushions on longer journeys. Fortunately times have improved beyond imagination since those pioneering days of eighty years ago, and the company still in the hands of the Rees family, operates the most modern of passenger vehicles.

93. Rees family members are pictured inside one of their coaches with founder Bert's sons Neville and Malcolm stood behind Neville's son and wife, Nigel and Margo.

CHAPTER 5

Clydach and Black Rock

94. Siloam Independent chapel Clydach which was built in 1829 following the first of a number of fervent and passionate religious Revivals that swept the area in 1828. The gentleman in the top hat is Reverend William Richards who was the minister in 1906. The chapel which was demolished in the 1970s, was close to the present-day Junior School and stood alongside the old tramroad; underneath the building was the caretaker's cottage, Mrs. Williams being the occupant for many years. The only remains to be found of the chapel now are quite a number of old and forgotten gravestones.

95. A Clydach scene from 1910 that shows the remains of the iron-works in the foreground. With all the ingredients for iron manufacture within close range, ore from Llanmarch mountainside (although the quality was not to be the best), limestone from Llangattock, wood for charcoal, before the use of coal and just as important, a plentiful supply of water, Clydach was the ideal setting for an ironworks. Once coal had been discovered in the area and with the huge advantage it had over charcoal for iron-smelting, mining levels were opened up all over the district, the Clydach valley having more than twenty in operation at one stage. The first undertaking for iron manufacture here was started as early as 1615 by the Hanbury family of Pontypool albeit on a small scale until 1793, when the works were taken over by Messers. Frere, Cooke and Co. and so began the transformation of a pure rural community to one of heavy industry. Rapid expansion took place with the formation of this new company and within a few years some 400 men were producing up to a hundred tons of finished metal a week with two blast furnaces and forges in operation. Not everything was as smooth as might be desired however, as industrial unrest amongst the men concerning general working conditions and in particular the hold that the ironmasters had over their livelihood with the truck shop system, was to blame for a series of strikes. A number of union clubs began to appear in the county, a prelude perhaps to the Chartist Movement, although it was said, that such 'clubs' were the work of militant immigrant English workers to the district rather than the local Welsh who were a little more accepting of things. Matters came to a head however in 1823, when a number of Clydach men, supported by their womenfolk, a number of whom were employed in gathering ore and working the levels, appeared before Brecon magistrates charged with assault and disorder and a rather threatening notice was put up for all to see at the ironworks which read as follows - *"How many times we gave notice to you about going in to work before you settle all together to go on better terms than were before or better than what you ask at present? Notice to you, David Thomas John and David Davies and Andrew Cross, that the Bull and his friends are all alive, and the vale of Llanmarch is wide, and woe shall be to you, since death you shall doubtless all have at once, you may depend on this. It may be that the might you don't expect we shall come again. We are not afraid were you to go all at once to work".* The notice was written in a mixture of English and Welsh suggesting that the 'blacklegs' might have been a mixture of both races and that not all militancy could be blamed on the so-called immigrant workers. The fortunes of Clydach ironworks were mixed in the ensuing years, one of a number of problems being the importation of iron ore from the continent that was double the quality and half the price, to say nothing of the new experiments with steel manufacture that were going on in nearby Blaenavon. Eventually the company could no longer compete in a dwindling market and their works at Clydach and also Beaufort were closed down in 1861.

96. The village in 1905, with the Wesleyan Chapel which was built in 1829 on the right, and next door was the village Post Office. At one time there were four nonconformist places of worship serving this part of Clydach including one for the Apostolics, a movement that took root in Brynmawr during the First World War. The Wesleyan is the last to survive whilst the Post Office is now a private house as is the former Apostolic building now called Highbury and built in 1821.

97. Situated close to the route of the old tramroad and above the expanse of the Clydach Valley rests Wood House, a somewhat secluded property but one that is steeped in history and one of the few remaining buildings to remind one of nineteenth-century architecture in the district. In 1806 there was born one John Jones who, when he reached manhood, worked for Crawshay Bailey as a master-blacksmith and plate-layer. He appears to have been a slightly introvert character and after marrying a local girl, decided that he did not wish to live and mix within a closed community, preferring a more secluded place of residence and one that he would have to build himself. On hearing this, the ironmaster presented his loyal employee with a piece of land beside the tramway running from Brynmawr to Llangattock and so Mr. Jones built Wood House in about 1832 and became one of the rare breed of workers owning their own land and property in the district. John Jones prospered under Crawshay Bailey and played an important part in the development and perfection of the 'T' shape design for railway track, this leading to him being put in charge of the valuable business of exporting rails to railway companies in Europe and America. (In Llanelly Churchyard will be found the grave of a relative William Jones with the 'T' head motif on the gravestone suggesting a close link with the rail's invention). He became the father of 7 sons and 2 daughters and the whole family over the years contributed in many ways to the evolution of Clydach village with two of his sons becoming nationally-recognized poets. The eldest, John junior, emigrated to the State of Pennsylvania in the U.S.A. in about 1855 which was then attracting thousands of Welsh immigrants throughout the 19th century during the emergence of its own iron and steel industry. (During the period of his emigration, the average intake of Welsh workers was 1,200 per year but in 1900, a colossal 100,000 journeyed there in just one year and a census taken at the time revealed that a third of all Welsh stock across America had settled in one State - Pennsylvania). There is today, a town in the State called Jonesville whose name is said to have derived from the early Clydach settler and his family and descendants are still to be found on the west coast State of California having of course paid a visit to Clydach in recent years researching their family history.

As can be seen in this photograph, the course of the 18th century tramroad lies directly in front of the house and what was once a small cottage, has been magnificently restored to modern-day standards and named Ty-yn-y-Coed (House In The Wood) with some breathtaking views at its disposal.

98. Ffynon-y-Coed, Black Rock at the turn of the 19th and 20th centuries and in the middle of the cottages on the right, was one of a number of former Clydach public houses, the Miners Arms which is nowadays a private dwelling 'Hen-Westy'. This road was the route of the former precipitous toll road that dropped sharply from Brynmawr's mountainous elevation of 400 metres to Gilwern's plateau of 120. An Act of Parliament was passed in 1767 to allow the setting up of a system of tolls, toll gates and houses in the county, the revenue from which was to be used for the maintenance and widening of existing roads and the development of new highways as and when required. The completion of the road between Brynmawr and Abergavenny, which was engineered by Mr. Henry Bailey, was seen as a great boost to coaching traffic, for by 1805 there was a service travelling from Milford Haven through Clydach Gorge to London five times a week; the distance and duration of that journey can only be imagined! Apart from usage by the coaches, many local farmers and traders were obliged to use this route, particularly as Brynmawr began to develop as a popular market town and it became a profitable venture. For the period, the tolls were considered exorbitant and unfair with charges of 4p for a horse drawing a carriage, $2^{1}/_{2}$p for a horse and cart and 1p for a single horse-rider. One major complaint recorded by road-users was that the horses of South Wales were far smaller and weaker than their English counterparts and consequently, could only haul much smaller loads whilst still having to pay the same rates of toll charges. In 1842 there was widespread discontent, disturbances and attacks on toll-gates throughout South Wales, incited by excessive charges, mismanagement of funds which were supposed to be used to improve the road system and a general aggressive attitude by the toll collectors. This led to the passing of a new South Wales Turnpike Act in 1844 which brought about much tighter controls of the toll system, passing responsibilities to each individual county who were directed to set up their own County Roads Board made up of magistrates, gentry and the like who might be considered more responsible. By 1862 the railway line had been opened between Abergavenny and Brynmawr, a major step forward in logistics, but not so good news for the toll-keepers, and thus the road through Clydach became less and less important. The passing by Parliament of the Local Government Act in 1888, which established County Councils for the first time, allowed local councils to assume authority over the highways and many of the laws governing the charges of road tolls were all but repealed to the relief of many.

99. Pictured in the 1960s is the former Royal Oak public house. The first building seen on the left was a carpenter's shop whilst the larger one which comprised of a cottage and an adjoining pub. The Royal Oak was kept by members of the same family for 62 years, firstly by John Dando, followed by his son Charlie. Mention must be made here of local character Mr. Jim Sharp, who during the 1940s and '50s took it upon himself to direct traffic through this part of the village, a particularly dangerous bend on what was then the main road from Brynmawr to Abergavenny. A Londoner by birth, he would be seen day in, day out, sat on the wall or on a chair provided by the Royal Oak ensuring safe passage for all, and for this undulating passion for road safety, he was created a 'Knight of the Road' by the News of the World newspaper.

100. The former Five Bells Inn far up on the mountainside and quite remote for a public house is pictured here in the 1960s. Situated directly opposite Llanelly Church, it adopted its name from the church, the tower of which contains five very antiquated bells. Long-closed, the inn is still easily recognisable having been expertly converted into private housing.

101. This picture illustrates what life was like for the villagers of Clydach before the opening of the Heads of The Valley Road. Mrs. Margaret 'Maggie' Dando stands on the steps of the Royal Oak as a Pickfords unit hauling a consignment bound for Ebbw Vale steelworks negotiates the bend. The Knight of the Road was not on duty on this occasion but Mr. George House is sat in his place observing the proceedings. The steps outside the pub on which Mrs. Dando stands were a problem in themselves as they would often be found the following morning a few yards further down the road having been hit by passing traffic!

102. A workman stands amidst the remains of what was a very old public house in this part of Clydach namely the Clydach Arms. Fire devastated the building on the night of April 19th 1912 (notice the old cast-iron oven where the fire may well have started) and the landlady at the time was Mrs. Leah Morgan. Such was the amount of damage that the building was abandoned for a number of years, never re-opening as a pub. Not that the village was deprived of such establishments for within easy walking distance, licensed premises included The Miners Arms, The Royal Oak, Rock and Fountain, Hafod Inn, Black Rock, Prince Albert, Unicorn, Alma and Bellevue. All that remain are the Rock and Fountain and the Prince Albert which has been renamed the Drum and Monkey. Although the Hafod still retains the original appearance of a public house, it is now a block of flats and most of the other buildings have been converted into private dwellings including the Royal Oak, appropriately named Oak House whilst the Miners has become a plentiful garden next to the former Ebenezer chapel.

103. Very few photographs exist of the tramroad that once ran the length of the valley down to the canal at Gilwern, but this view of 1899 provides some idea of the scene that was begun in 1794 as the main route for the transportation of minerals and iron before the arrival of the railways some 70 years later. Vital limestone was brought by mule-hauled trams on an eight-mile stretch of track from the Llangattock quarries and when the ironworks of Beaufort and Nantyglo were working at their peak, it was claimed that there were almost 300 miles of tramroad above and below ground serving the companies.

104. Rose Cottage, a secluded dwelling that stood overlooking the upper reaches of the River Clydach, opposite a former picturesque landmark Pont Harry Isaac bridge; this part of the river causing great concern to the residents of Clydach during the first half of the nineteenth century due to high pollution. At this time Brynmawr was without a drainage, sewerage or proper water system and the river was used as a main discharge for effluent despite years of protest and exasperation by the residents of Clydach. Following a serious outbreak of cholera in 1847, the authorities finally acted and the first Board of Health was formed in the district to alleviate the situation. A sewage system was installed at Brynmawr in the 1850s although not with total efficiency for another sixty years or so, with contamination from leaking pipework finding its way into a number of springs and wells which older inhabitants still used as their water supply. Typhoid was still a killer disease in the area until 1925 before the whole sewage system was replaced.

105. Some communication that has survived since April 1895 between Clydach quarry owners and their coal supplier at Beaufort, requesting that coal wagons be accounted for and advising that the lime is on its way. As the quarry company owned their own wagons, they were concerned that they should not find their way into main line traffic and end up being lost for months at a time.

106. A view looking towards Brynmawr from the platforms of the former London and North Western station at Gilwern in about 1920. The station was busy enough to employ a stationmaster who is seen on the right and according to the signals, trains are expected in both directions.

107. Govilon station with a goods train passing through a peaceful setting whilst the country was at war in July 1941. The much-longed-for rail link between Abergavenny and Brynmawr opened on September 29th 1862 with Govilon being the only stop until stations were added later at Gilwern and Clydach. The privilege of driving the first train (with some professional assistance) as far as Govilon, was given to Mrs. Hill, wife of the railway company's vice-chairman, probably the only occasion when a female engine driver was allowed to do so on this line!

108. The area of Black Rock with a number of buildings that have since disappeared. Lower centre is the garage of Alf Chivers the former bus and haulage firm with Ynys-y-Garth (old ironworks to the right). In the centre are a few more for locals to remember such as Siloam chapel, the original Primary School which was opened as early as 1866 and the Police House.

109. The main road link between Brynmawr and Abergavenny through Clydach as it appeared in the 1950s and it's hard to believe that drivers of double decked buses could manoeuvre the route so well. Remains of the old tramroad can just be seen to the right of the bus.

CHAPTER 6
Social Activity and Events

110. The first section of the open air swimming pool shortly after opening in 1930. Note that there is still much work to be done in removing the ash tips in the background.

The plight of Brynmawr and its jobless inhabitants during the 1920s and '30s is nowadays very difficult to imagine and is all but forgotten in this age of a Welfare State. Between 1920 and 1930 the Country's political and industrial scene was one of turmoil. It saw the last Liberal government, a first Labour government, a despised-by-many Conservative government and finally a National Coalition. The year of the first ever General Strike in 1926 was about the time when depression set in around Brynmawr, and a desire to regenerate the town became a focus of attention. Apart from the obvious need, the creation of jobs, there was also a social side of life to consider and one of the first suggestions put forward was for the construction of a park and playground facilities. This project was financed in the main by the Miners' Welfare Fund and was developed in 1928 after draining an old feeder pond to Nantyglo Ironworks. By now however, the economic slump had truly set in and the only hope of any further development in the area could be through the recruitment of voluntary unpaid labour and so began a venture that was to become known as 'The Brynmawr Experiment'. The first offer of help arrived from the town of Worthing in Sussex (it taking upon itself to 'morally adopt' Brynmawr in its hour of need) suggested by a committee belonging to the Society of Friends (Quakers), an informal Christian sect that was founded in the middle of the 17th century by George Fox; led by prominent figures in the denomination Peter Scott and Lord Jim Forrester, their local headquarters were at 31 Alma Street. Further invaluable assistance came in 1929 with the arrival of a small group of Welsh voluntary Christian students, later to be added to in greater numbers by overseas supporters as mentioned in an earlier chapter. Appreciative as they were of this outside help in resurrecting the town, a number of local unemployed volunteer workers now began to question their own part joining the scheme. Firstly there was the fear of losing their unemployment benefit which deterred many from offering their time, although this was soon disproved by a test case. Then there was the matter of Trade Union principles, whereby it was argued that the movement's bargaining powers regarding pay and conditions would be totally undermined in the area if such voluntary working practices were to spread.

This point put serious thought into the minds of many local men, quite a number of whom decided against offering their free labour but nevertheless the enterprise went ahead without recourse. The first task was to remove a large waste tip and clear a derelict area of 5¹/₂ acres ready for the construction of a bowling green, tennis courts and a substantial outdoor swimming pool. After sustained fundraising, willpower and two years hard labour, the initial swimming baths were finally opened by the Duchess of Beaufort in July 1932. The park and pool were further improved and extended in 1937 with the help of a government Special Areas Grant, making it one of the most used facilities in the area at the time attracting up to 20,000 bathers a year and a bank balance of just 13 pence in 1932, had turned into a most profitable undertaking. Recognising this, the Urban District Council took over responsibility for all the park amenities from the founders' committee shortly before the outbreak of war in 1939. These days little has survived of this particular chapter of 'The Brynmawr Experiment' other than the bowling green which is actively used by the town's club.

111. A photograph from the latter end of the 1930s with Windsor Road in the background and it can now be seen that further improvements to the pool have been completed.

An extract from an appeal leaflet distributed around the area in 1931.

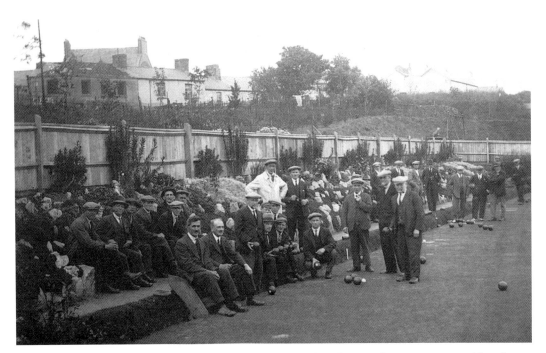

112. Another view from the 1930s with fellow bowlers and spectators amidst the rockery and green. There is a distinct absence of ladies in this photograph suggesting that they had not yet taken up this ancient and noble game.

113. The tennis courts in the Welfare Grounds as they appeared shortly after opening some seventy years ago. One court is still in use, the other having been re-designed for the use of skateboards.

114. A Brynmawr County School cricket team with members from Brynmawr, Clydach and Gilwern posing for a photographer in 1932 with headmaster Mr. Price in the trilby hat and to his right, the only other name to have been traced unfortunately is Jack Haley.

115. A soccer team from the former Semtex factory and some names have been recalled as follows - Back: Len Williams, Joe Wall, Mike Watkiss, Gary Nicklin, unknown, unknown, unknown, Selwyn Ford and 'Mecca' Watkins. Front: Jeff Smith, Roland Parfitt, Alan Williams, Mike Morris, Alva Williams and Mike Davies.

116. Part of a Brynmawr Scouts football team who are seen here in 1948 and the players include G. Morgan, S. Haynes, E. Howells, T. Walbyoff and R. Lewis.

117. The Rover Scouts AFC team in 1949 that includes the following - Back: D. Hill, K. Landman, D. Tucker, J. Morgan, E. George, R. Parfitt and F. Hapgood. Front: G. Jennings, A. Knight, P. Phillips, D. Amos and D. Haynes.

118. A Semtex team pictured before an inter-factory competition game and most of the players' names have been traced as follows - Back: Jeff Smith, Don Phillips, George Bishop, Alan Tovey, Daryl Best, Monty Lewis, Chris Morris, Lyn Walters and Ivor Williams. Front: Selwyn Ford, unknown, Malcolm Snellgrove, Malcolm Paull, Ken Rossiter, Dennis Morgan and Len Williams.

119. A final soccer-related photograph with the Dunlop Semtex team and club members at Coventry for the 1965-66 inter-factory cup final. To be seen are C. Jones, J. Wall, N. Bird, M. Paull, Ken Rossiter, C. Nock, W. Morris, L. Walters, D. Jones, M. Snellgrove and Keith Rossiter.

120. This time it's the turn of Brynmawr's rugby club to get a mention, having been in the business since 1892 and playing well enough to have joined the Welsh Rugby Union and Monmouthshire League three years later. In this picture, left to right are - Back: R. Brimble (trainer), N. Mathews, J. Brooks, D. Withers, B. Rees, P. Knapp, D. Chappel, B. Meyrick, J. Gore, T. Walbyoff (Sec.), M. Hughes, G. Isaac, D. McCann, K. John, K. Harty, S. Tippens (Coach). Front: B. Arnold, B. Whatley, C. Hillman, M. Beynon (Chairman), P. Beynon (Capt.), B. Harry (Mayor Blaenau Gwent), A. Knapp, N. Strange, B. Parry.

121. The present Queen's Silver Jubilee was held in June 1977 with the usual celebrations taking place all over the country. Here the parents and children mainly from the Glamorgan Street area celebrate the event indoors.

122./123. A rather unusual event took place in Brynmawr in October 1953 when a light aircraft was forced to ditch in the Waun Pond near the Semtex factory. The pilot was Mr. John Collins the proprietor of the funfair at Barry Island who ran into trouble over the town, and thanks to the help of local schoolboy Lyndon Humphries and friends, was rescued. These two rare photographs show the recovery of the aircraft underway. As it happens, this was not the first near-disaster in the skies over Brynmawr. On May 22nd 1944, within the last year of World War Two, a crew of seven R.A.F. men of Bomber Command survived when they were forced to abandon their Halifax Mk.III whilst on a training flight over the area from Humberside. A severe oil leak and sudden engine failure brought the aircraft down into the peat bog surrounding the old Milfraen Colliery at Waunavon.

82

124./125. Two photographs that reflect a carnival spirit from days gone by. The upper scene is from the 1920s and was taken in King Street where most of the houses in the background have since taken on a new look. Below the period is about 1910 and this time the event is taking place in Bailey Street, close to the chapel. Some readers may remember Cammermans fruit and vegetable shop which was situated at this spot.

126. The legendary Welsh Folk Dancers of Brynmawr who were never short of enthusiasm in preserving their heritage. Led by such familiar names as Rendall Davies, Marie Thomas (of Marie's Café fame), Ralph Gould and many more, they performed and competed all over Wales. This particular photograph was taken in the 1950s.

127. Calling themselves 'The Welsh Reel' these performers are pictured in 1950 and some names can be remembered as follows: Mr. Maurice Jones (Ex Headmaster of the Senior School) - far left, Miss Griffiths - far right, Miss Phillips - centre. Also in the group are Ron Baker, Myra Langford, Olive Upham, John Hughes, Mary Davies, Roslyn Roberts and Clive Prout.

128. Members and guests of The St. John Ambulance Brigade on the steps of their headquarters, the Mission Church. At the back is superintendent Mr. Thomas, front left is Bill Perry and the other uniformed officer is Mr. Hunt. The St. John Organisation is an ancient one, its foundations being formed in Jerusalem, in the 12th century by a group of monks caring for sick pilgrims; flourishing across Europe, it was dormant for centuries after having been banned by Henry VIII. Resurrected in 1877 as a totally voluntary body, by 1887 it had spread its good work throughout the country with Brynmawr being the second oldest division formed in Wales, that occurring in 1898.

129. The exact date of this photograph taken outside the Market Hall is May 7th 1910 and even in those days it will be seen that a travelling fairground sometimes occupied the square. Before the arrival of radio, television and so on, public announcements of great importance were made from the local town halls and in progress here is the proclamation of King George V following the death of Edward VII.

130. Something much looked-forward-to a few years back was the Brynmawr Youth Club's annual camp which is recorded here near Aberystwyth in 1952 and as best that can be remembered, some names are as follows: Back: Richard Lewis, Lance Huxley, Olive Davies, Josie Jones, Gaye, Rosemary Jones, Nan, Monica, Eirwen, Janice. 2nd row: ?, ?, ?, Gwenyth, Ron Mayrick, Clive James, Mary, Diana, Myra, Mr. Thompson. 3rd row: Mostyn, Mr. Preece, Mrs. Preece, Mrs. Richards, Rhoda, Mr. Evans, Mr.Richards, Jean, Graham, Joan. Front: Clive, Goronwy, Dennis, Clive, David, Bobby, Ron, Enos, Melwyn, Maurice, David.

131. The First World War ended on November 11th 1918 and a memorial service has been held on the nearest Sunday to that date ever since. This picture shows the official unveiling of Brynmawr's cenotaph on a wet morning of October 30th 1927, some nine years after the war ended. The series of books First World War Graves and Memorials in Gwent by Ray Westlake are to be recommended for more comprehensive details on the subject.

CHAPTER 7

Matters of Religion and Learning

132. The 1930s were still heady days as far as religion was concerned in Brynmawr, as to be witnessed by this procession that stretches down the biggest part of Beaufort Street and attracts a large audience.

133. Holy Trinity Church which was consecrated on 10th August 1854, was on the borders of the parishes of Aberystruth and Llanelly and technically in the ecclesiastical district of Nantyglo. It was the brainchild of industrialist Crawshay Bailey who, recognising the growing numbers of nonconformists and the chapels they were erecting in the area, and the fact that Brynmawr was without its own church, felt that the location of Holy Trinity would attract enthusiastic congregations from both towns and stem the tide. In later years it was to be almost engulfed by the building of the Semtex factory, all of which has now disappeared.

134. A late 1920s picture of religious fervour on Brynmawr's square depicting a banner-carrying parade by St. Mary's Church. For the church, the annual march was a two-day event held on the first Sunday and Monday in July with processions of witness led by the Town Silver Band as seen here. The clergyman, just visible in front of the banner, is believed to be Reverend Frederick Oswell who was vicar for an exceptional thirty years.

135. Llanelly Church which is perched high on the mountainside overlooking Gilwern and the valley some three miles from Brynmawr itself, originally served as the parish church for the town. In the second half of the 19th century, it was developing at a pace and with a population approaching 5,000, the approval of new boundaries led to the formation of the new parish of Brynmawr in June 1875.

136. An interior of the church taken in about 1920. An age-old place of worship, much has been preserved of its long past including the Parish Register which dates from 1701 with early entries in Latin. Major restoration took place in 1868 including a new burial ground, but by 1896 even more expensive work was needed in building a completely new spire and repairs to the tower for its ancient bells, the largest of which was cast in the mid 1400s and said to have been used in a monastery before finding its way to Llanelly.

137. Regretted by some, church and chapel walks and parades now seem to be out of fashion, with Christian religious beliefs not enjoying the enthusiasm they once did. This scene also provides some interesting background detail as the walkers pass the King's Head Inn on the corner of Beaufort Street and King Street whilst next door, more moderate forms of liquid refreshment could be found inside Henry Williams' Coffee House.

138. The background scenery in this photograph is not so easily recognisable, it being at the junction of King Street and the top of George Street. For some reason the timing of Sunday School and Chapel walks in Brynmawr was distinct, it being first Monday in July and not the traditional Whitsun Monday as shared by virtually all other valley towns. The dress fashion suggests the period to be around 1910.

139. The choirboys of St. Mary's Church proceed down King Street. The first St. Mary's Church was consecrated in January 1872, the foundation stone having been laid initially by Mr. Crawshay Bailey, one of his last public duties before his death on 9th January 1872. The church was beset with financial difficulties from the start, with Bailey coming to the rescue with the signature from his death-bed of a blank cheque to clear a bundle of debts which had risen to almost £1,000 a substantial sum indeed for the year 1872. Far worse was to come a few years later in 1891, when an architect's report brought bad news, stating the building to be unsafe due to poor foundations, rotting timbers and dampness throughout; whereas such buildings had lasted for centuries, St. Mary's was crumbling in less than twenty years, having to be pulled down in 1899. Undaunted however, the parishioners saw a future and toiled relentlessly until sufficient funds were raised to build a completely new church which was consecrated in July 1900. Constructed by Brynmawr's builder John Jenkins of King Street, using quantities of locally quarried stone, the church was at last a structure of some quality and still stands sound, more than a hundred years on.

140. A view of the church in about 1903 not long after its re-construction and in the background is the vicarage. Even the building of this caused concern to the church members, with the contractor going bankrupt half way through the work and the then vicar Rev. Phillips having to wait two years before finally taking up residence in August 1888.

141./142. Two photographs that further record past enthusiasm for the chapel walk around the town, both of which are of members of Calvary Baptist in King Street. Above, the ladies are assembled outside the chapel in 1934 and below, the girls belonging to the Sunday School wear their 'Sunday best' as they walk down Beaufort Street in the 1960s.

143. The Salvation Army Citadel as it looked in King Street in 1908 and although the original building is still there, it has taken on a more-modern look and is these days the home of the Apostolic Church. Formed in 1865, the Salvationist movement came to Brynmawr during the 1880s with meetings and activities held in the barracks seven days a week and a rapturous open-air service held at the bottom of Queen Street every Saturday evening, such was their vigour. By the turn of the century it was just one of thirteen different religious denominations to choose from in the town.

144. The interior of St. Mary's Catholic Church in the 1950s. Long before Brynmawr's evolution as a leading Breconshire town, the county was one of the very few places in Wales where Catholicism survived the 16th century persecutions following Henry VIII's breaking with Rome and his self-appointment as supreme head of the Church of England. St. Mary's Church and a day school for the education of the faith's young was opened in 1863, some nine years before the building of the first Anglican church.

145. This photograph of a religious gathering goes to these followers who are making their way up King Street returning for a traditional 'after walk tea' to be served at Calvary Chapel during the 1950s.

146. A flock from St. Mary's passes by what was the entrance to the old Griffin Hotel at the top of Beaufort Street, it becoming vacant after the opening of the new one at the bottom of the street. St. Mary's, with the help of a number of businessmen and the bank, seized the opportunity to buy the building in 1919 and whilst a little large for their own use, part of it was sold to the local Co-operative Society. To be known as 'Church House' it served as a profitable centre of social activity for many years but nowadays and with the ornate entrance long-since-removed, it is the British Legion Club.

147. Members of Bethesda Chapel are in full song at the bottom of Beaufort Street in 1949. Amongst the crowd are Church Secretary Mr. Walbyoff, Mr. W. Griffin, Mrs. W. Stone, Miss M. Hopkins, Miss M. Lewis and Mrs. Griffin.

148. A selection of pupils and staff at the Comprehensive School in 1983 and whilst space does not permit a complete list of names, the headmaster Mr. Scott-Archer is in the front row far right. A few other members of staff amongst the crowd are Jim Beddoe, Martin Preece and Mr. Bromwell.

The following four pages are devoted to photographs taken at Brynmawr Bi-Lateral School in May 1960 and where possible, staff and pupils' names have been provided in alphabetical order, with sincere apologies for any errors or omissions.

Staff: R. Atkins, R. Alexander, G. Bowen, Tim Craven, Mr. Crewe, Wyn Davies, A. Ford, Miss Griffin, Miss Griffiths, H. Havard, Miss Howells, Margaret Hewins, Mr. James, Miss Jenkins, Ken Jones, Rowley Jones, R. Knowles, Mrs. Lewis, Mr. Lloyd, Carol Morgan, E. Morgan, Mr. J. Morgan, Joe Morgan, Miss Morris, S. Pearce, Miss Rees, Mr. Beddoe-Rees, Mr. Suff, Mr. Thomas, E. Watkins, Albert White, Miss Wilkins, Harry Williams.

Pupils: Yvonne Arnold, Stefan Aylett, Wynford Aylett, Yvonne Arnold, Barbara Bailey, Sheila Baker, Pauline Ball, Graham Barnes, Pat Bedford, Philip Bedford, Jocelyn Bevan, Sandra Bond (2), Glenys Bowen, Peter Bull, Kay Brown, Malcolm Brown, Terry Brown, Tyrone Brown, Russell Bull, Howard Bush, Angela Caffarelli, Rosalind Collier, Diane Collett, Roger Collett, Roger Collier, Gary Cunvin, Janet Cross, Ann Dancey, David Davies, Malcolm Davies, Margaret Davies, Myra Davies, Peter Dennington, Brian Dowding, Margaret Duffy, Martin Duffy, Jimmy Dyer, Diane Embling, Colin Edmund, Meryl Edmund, Lyn Etheridge, Barry Evans, Croes Evans, Glyn Evans, Nora Evans, Rosamund Evans, Marie Excell, Norman Excell, Haydn Eynon, John Fennesey, Janice Forbes, Ruth Francis, Peter Furber, Hugh Garrett, Ian Garrett, Irene Gore, Russell Gore, Ann Gould, Pat Gould, Martin Greatwood, John Griffiths, Pamela Griffiths, Pat Griffin, Joy Gunter, Kerry Gunter, Maureen Gunter, Rosemary Hamilton, Daphne Harvey, Susan Herbert, Graham Hill, Jennifer Hobbs, Lyn Hodge, Robin Hoffman, Terry Hoffman, John Hopkins, Pauline Howells, Christine Hughes, John Hughes, Pat Hughes, Susan Hughes (2), Malcolm Humphries, Helen and Vivienne James, Lyn James, Jennifer Jenkins, Sandra Jeremy, Clive Jones, David Jones, Derek Jones, Gwyllis Jones, Haydn Jones, Josephine and Christine Jones, Linda Jones, Philip Jones, Royston Jones, Yvonne Jones, Ann Jordan, John Keeling, Valerie Keen, Marlene Kelly, Madison Kelso, Janet King, Clive Knock, Colin Lewis, Derek Lewis, Gwyn Lewis, Gwynvil Lewis, Lorraine Lewis, Ivor Lewis, Sandra Lewis, Francis Long, Lucius Marshman, Alan McCloy, Gerald McCloy, David Meredith, Glenyn Meredith, Jacqueline Meredith, Karen Meredith, David Miles, Jill Miles, Lyn Miles, Doris Mills, Lily Mills, David Mogford, Clive Morgan, David Morgan, Geraldine Morgan, Jacky Morgan, Jacqueline Morgan, Leslie Morgan, Lyn Morgan, Malcolm Morgan, Michael Morgan, Roger Morgan, Ann Morrell, Jean Morris, Pam Morris, Sandra Mortimer, Barry Mower, Michael Noble, Byron Norman, Katherine O'Keefe, Winona Owen, Royston Packer, Barry Paige, Sandra Paige, David Parfitt, June Parfitt, Jennifer Parry, Ray Parry, Ronnie Phillips, Ann Philpotts, Ruth Pinkney, Margaret Powell, Geoffrey Presdee, Janet Price, Jill Price, Robert Price, Ian Ransome, June Reames, David Rees, Ilfryn Rees, Judith Beddoe-Rees, Lyndon Rees, Marie Rees, Wayne Rice, Michael Rigby, Terry Rigby, Jennifer Roberts, Nesta Roberts, Rita Roberts, Selwyn Roberts, Marilyn Roderick, Christine Seaward, Phyllis Seswick, Jeffrey Sims, David Skull, John Smith, Neil Smith, Mary Starr, Ken Street, Howard Swales, Barbara Thomas, Billy Thomas, Christine Thomas, David Thomas, Glyn Thomas, Janet Thomas, Lance Thomas, Clive Thrupp, Jane Timmins, Pam Trivett, Alan Walby, Margaret Walbyoff, David Walters, Kay Washbrook, Barry Waters, David Watkins, Dennis Watkins, Tudor Watkins, Gwynfor Webley, Margarita Webley, Verdun Webley, Audrey Westall, Jimmy Wiggins, Terry Wiggins, Janet White, Brian Williams, Colin Williams, Corrine Williams, Diane Williams, Mary Williams, Merlyn Williams, Michael Williams, Pamela Williams, Peter Williams, Robert Williams (2), Roy Williams, Michael Woodyatt, Jennifer Young, Ken Young, Lyndon Young, Sandra Young.

149. /150. During the period of this series of photographs, the early 1960s, the first Labour Government for thirteen years introduced their long written manifesto concerning secondary education. The two-tier system of grammar and secondary modern schools, decided by the 11 Plus Exam, was gradually phased out to be replaced by the all-embracing comprehensive scheme that we know today.

151./152. The former Secondary Modern School in Clydach Street was merged with what was originally known as The County School (opened in 1897) to form the Bi-Lateral School, the building being used until demolition in the 1970s and the first step in modernising secondary education in the town. At this stage a completely new Comprehensive School was built on a new site, the original grounds being used to construct St. Mary's Church in Wales Primary School at Intermediate Road.

153./154. Schooling in the area for the first three-quarters of the nineteenth century was in the main, conducted by the clergy, particularly the nonconformist followers who held classes at their own expense in private cottages and various chapels as they steadily began to appear around Brynmawr. The fact that the nonconformists were beginning to dominate early education in Wales, led to an investigation and a damning report supported by embittered Anglican clerics in 1847 caused resentment throughout the principality for many years thereafter.

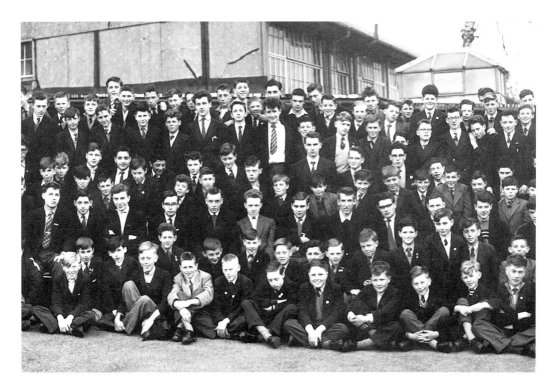

155. /156. The Education Act of 1870 did at last bring things to order, providing powers to enforce school attendance for all classes of children up to the age of thirteen, although not totally free of charge; at the age of fourteen however, they were expected to be fully employed and supporting the family, regardless of sex. The Act was welcomed with open arms in Brynmawr with the setting-up of a local Board led by Mr. John Thomas, the town's long-serving social stalwart, resulting in the building of a commodious school in King Street in 1876.

CHAPTER 8

Brynmawr Then and Now

157./158. Just a week after the closure of Brynmawr's station this 'special' brought parties of steam buffs up the western valley from Newport on May 6th 1962, a day of pleasure and great regret. Some forty years on and looking in the direction of the Semtex factory, the joy of rail travel has been totally eradicated to be replaced by what we see below.

159./160. Two photographs that illustrate how time has changed the face of another little corner of Brynmawr. This is the corner junction of Worcester Street and Glamorgan Street that once housed the White Lion pub, subsequently demolished to make way for a Social Services centre seen in the bottom picture some forty years on.

161./162. Another 'disappeared' public house with the familiar Hobby Horse sign belonging to the Rhymney and Crosswell brewery is the New Inn which was at No.90 King Street. As will be seen, the building has since been transformed into an attractive private dwelling.

163./164. The Dunlop Semtex factory seen in 1963 and the picture as it looked forty years later. For numerous reasons, particularly a chronic shortage of skilled labour and materials after six years war with Germany, it took another five long years to complete the rubber factory project, eventually to be hailed as ones of Britain's masterpieces of industrial architecture. Ironically, much of the technology for the construction of the famed domed concrete roofs was copied freely from the conquered nation after its collapse in 1945.

165. Above is the factory complex during the 1960s, the lakeside location providing an attractive outlook from the office block. Four and a half years after closure and a long campaign, the factory and its boiler house which stood on the opposite side of the main road were declared by government to be buildings of great industrial history and granted Grade II listing, the first post-war building to receive this high status. This proved to be a decision that the local council and development planners could have well done without, the move leading to years of debate and indecision as to what could be done with the site.

166. This is how it all looked at the end of 2003, the only remaining evidence being the pump house that was used to extract water from the lake into the factory.

167./168. Another building with a long and mixed history is number 16 Market Square, formerly known as Victoria Buildings. Formerly the furniture shop of Messrs. Powell and Jones, it is seen here in the 1960s when it was the offices of the Red and White Bus Co. who earlier, had acquired Tom Jones's Griffin Bus Co. As will be seen, the building is now a branch of Travellers World and Bailey Street Chapel in the background has disappeared, it having been demolished in 1970.

169. Here is the former boot factory in Warwick Road. Boots, mainly for industrial use with the familiar Gwalia trademark had been manufactured in Brynmawr since 1850 by Mr. George Hicks, a Bristol shopkeeper and renowned upholder of moral standards in the town, an attribute that earned him the unofficial title of 'King of Brynmawr'. Although liquidated amidst the coal-mining depression of the early 1920s, the business was however revived in 1929 by a small group of unemployed men, who with local financial backing and support from the newly formed Brynmawr and Clydach Valley Industries Ltd., opened premises in Factory Road before moving to Warwick Road in 1937. Boots and shoes continued to be made in the town up until 1995 at the Tuf factory before that site also closed and moved to Blaina.

170. This is the scene at Warwick Road today, the old boot factory having been demolished to be replaced by the Bert Denning Centre providing occupational therapy for those with special needs within the community. The centre was opened by the first Secretary of the National Assembly for Wales, Alun Michael in October 1999.

171./172. The conclusion of this section of the book dealing with Brynmawr, comes with the earliest years of the twentieth century and the earliest years of the twenty-first century, the scene for comparison being the town's Market Square. A solitary oil or gas lamp standard for the whole of the square has been superseded by high powered electric lighting and another sign of the times in which we live - a closed circuit camera.

Beaufort

The town of Beaufort can be said to have been established in the year 1779 with the opening of its first ironworks, until which time it was a mere moorland district within the mineral-rich parishes of Llangattock and Llangynidr. This land was in the possession of nobleman, the Duke of Beaufort, he having inherited it from his ancestors the Earls of Worcester, one-time occupiers of Raglan Castle. The duke granted a 99-year lease to two entrepreneur brothers Edward and Jonathan Kendall that they be allowed to extract all the necessary ingredients from his ground and construct a furnace for the manufacture of iron. The agreed rent was set at £406 per annum, with additional royalties to be paid based on whatever volumes of output could be achieved. Another condition imposed by the duke, with early environmental issues in mind and anxious that his land should not become completely tarnished by industry, was that the brothers should *'guarantee each year to plant ten trees and fifty yards of hedgerows within their boundaries'*; a penalty of 25p and 12^{1}/2p respectively was levied for non-compliance with his demands! In its earliest of days before proper development into a populated town, the area was to be known as Kendall or Cendl (Welsh) so named after the newly-arrived ironmasters, the name Beaufort not being officially adopted until about 1800.

173. The lower half of Beaufort Rise in 1912 and on the right, with its sunblind down is a branch of the Blaina Industrial and Provident Co-operative Society and a little further up was one belonging to a competitor, the Ebbw Vale Society. For a period lasting well into the nineteenth century, the housewife's shopping options were few, and under the control of the ironmasters and their 'Company Shops' with hugely inflated prices. Beaufort however was luckier than most in the area, being under the ownership of the Kendall family it was acknowledged to be the only one with a genuine reputation for offering food and clothing at the fairest prices in appreciation of its workforce. The Co-op building seen here may also be remembered as Penry Davies the gents' hairdresser, it since having been demolished to make way for a car park. On the opposite side of the road was Roberts the bakers and grocers.

174. The Beaufort Arms and a rather roughshod highway as seen in the year 1902. The first public road was cut through this part of the mountainside by an Act of Parliament in 1815 although to be controlled by tollgates erected at the top of the hill and lower down at Rhyd-y-Blew. Just below where the young boy stands and on the left is Beaufort's long established shop belonging to the Carini family.

175. A picture taken on The Rise in 1905 and on the right is one of Beaufort's numerous public houses from that period namely The Greyhound which at the time was in the care of Mr. George Bromley. What were shops on the left are now private houses whilst further down on the right, the corner building is today's Post Office (an amenity that has seen five different locations over the years).

176. This photograph taken at Rassau in 1920, clearly shows the old tramline still in place, it originally having been built in the late eighteenth century and used for the haulage of limestone from the plentiful Trevil quarries to feed Ebbw Vale ironworks which had been in production since 1788. Residential flats and bungalows have now replaced the nineteenth-century cottages on the left of the picture.

177. Church District or Carmeltown in the early part of the twentieth century with a few familiar buildings that still stand today. The corner of the graveyard of Carmel Welsh Congregational Chapel (re-built in 1865 and now a Grade II Listed Building) is to be seen which contains resting places dating back 150 years, a number of its gravestones inscribed in Welsh, it being the preferred tongue through much of the nineteenth century. Upper left is Needhams Row and on the right is Price's shop.

178. Crawshay Bailey a powerful and forceful ironmaster was also a generous benefactor, particularly when it came to the encouragement of religious beliefs amongst his workforce. Demolished some years ago, this is the original Beaufort parish church of St. John the Evangelist, which was built with the compliments of the Bailey Company at a cost of almost £1600 in 1843 with sittings for 250 worshippers. Beaufort was formed into a completely new ecclesiastical district in September 1846 from the civil parishes of Llangattock and Llangynidir in Breconshire and Aberystruth and Bedwellty in Monmouthshire and whilst the town had cried out for a parish church, it was not actually consecrated for another thirty years. The chosen site for the building of this church however was not a good one; in the first instance the landscape in this part of Beaufort gradually became extremely unstable following years of nearby mineral and industrial workings. Criticisms were made public within a relatively short time of its opening that it was of poor design and workmanship, falling far short of what Crawshay Bailey had intended. Consisting of a nave, north porch and an embattled single-bell tower, the appearance began to deteriorate alarmingly until being declared unsafe and eventually condemned in 1890. By this time plans were already afoot with the construction of a new parish church, much lower down on flatter and safer territory, that of St. David's which was opened in 1891 and still stands well. St. John's was not abandoned totally however, with occasional services and burials held there for quite a number of years thereafter, in fact, the walled graveyard seen in this photograph was at one time the final resting place for more than 2,000 souls. There is however said to be one restless soul, that of a young mother whose ghostly figure with her babe in arms walks the area from time to time. The story goes that she is an abandoned wife whose father placed a curse on her unfaithful husband as an act of revenge, that was to lead to a tragic outcome. Mother and child were found mysteriously drowned in a nearby stream, whilst the sinful and cursed husband was lost at sea! The photograph above is from about 90 years ago and overlooks much, yet to be developed in the areas of Glyncoed and Badminton Grove Ebbw Vale and immediately in front of the church building numerous bungalows have since been constructed.

179. A panoramic view of Beaufort looking northwards during the 1920s with the smoking stack belonging to Beaufort Pipe and Brick Company in the background, a familiar landmark for over forty years. There is much evidence to be seen of new housing being built around Church View, Yard Row and Valley View on what was ravaged land and waste tips. In the lower right of the scene is Tyr Meddyg farm where the Pant-y-Fforest Estate now lies.

180./181. Two views from two different eras that show just some of the effects that the building of the Heads of the Valley Road has had on this part of Beaufort. The picture above was taken overlooking Llangynidr Road in about 1950 with the reservoir, housing and brickworks all in position; the row of 'temporary houses' were built of timber and known as Brickwork Huts. The lower photograph was taken in 1964, just a few days after the official opening of the A465 and the construction of a new road bridge onwards to Llangynidr. Some forty years later, the volume of traffic has quadrupled necessitating yet more major changes to the area.

182. The London Midland and Scottish railway station Beaufort in the 1920s with a passenger train heading in the direction of Brynmawr. Up until February 1951, before the branch line was closed to passenger traffic, travellers had the opportunity here to change trains on the route between Brynmawr and Merthyr and continue on a journey to Ebbw Vale High Level. The buildings in the top left were formerly known as Railway Houses.

183. This time the camera points in the opposite direction looking at the road bridge, signal box and goods yard in the background. The left-hand side platform housed the timber-made waiting room for passengers heading for Brynmawr and Abergavenny, whilst the main station building on the right, for those travelling in the direction of Merthyr or Ebbw Vale, was a sturdy stone construction. The roof of the theatre may be seen to the right of the bridge.

184. This is how parts of Beaufort looked in 1920 with the Beaufort Arms on the left, Railway Cottages centre (since demolished) and Soar Chapel right. In the distance is The Domen, an area used as an observation post during World War Two.

185./186. Two views of Rassau from yesteryear that illustrate many changes yet to come. Above, Graig Ebbw now occupies the area on the left whilst Rhyd-y-Cae is to the right. In the lower view a number of older buildings have since been demolished whilst a survivor, the Red Lion public house is to be seen in both photographs. Distantly in the bottom picture may be seen a prominent white house that used to belong to the popular medical practitioner Doctor Brooks.

187. A view taken from Garnlydan looking down Reservoir Road at Lower Cwm. In the distance is Waun-y-Pound and notably the absence of such newer landmarks as Ebbw Vale College, Hospital and Badminton Grove. Just beyond Vine Cottages in the centre was the works of the Beaufort Gas, Light and Coke Company keeping the town well-alight whilst much of the grassed area has now been replaced by modern housing.

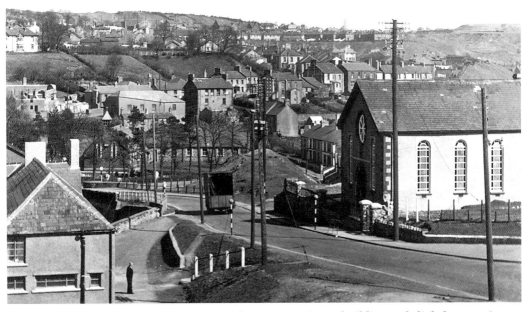

188. The period is the early 1950s with two prominent buildings of slightly opposing principles in view. On the left is the Ryd-y-Blew, once a nineteenth-century coaching inn and still open for business whilst Barham English Congregational Chapel which was built in 1875 on the other side of the road, has since been demolished.

189. The Greyhound Inn which has been trading on the hill for more than a hundred years. This picture however was taken in 1960 and at the time, the landlord would be able to serve a patron with a pint of best, 20 Woodbine cigarettes and a packet of plain crisps all for the princely sum of 4/4d - just under 22p!

190. The Rhyd-y-Blew which has taken on a much different look since this 1950s photograph. Having stood for more than 200 years, it was frequented by the Duke of Beaufort and his entourage before commencing their grouse-shoots on the nearby moors and also served as the meeting place for the town's first Friendly Society in the year 1810. Following an Act of Parliament in 1793, such Societies were greatly encouraged amongst the industrial population as a means of providing some benefits for the sick and old in the absence of sympathy and assistance from wealthier employers of the day.

191. Sub-postmaster Mr. Joseph Price and members of his family and staff stand outside the Post Office when it was situated at number 54, The Rise in the early 1900s. A telephone system not having been available in Beaufort at this time, made this office was a very busy and important centre for the public to send and receive telegraphic communication, it having to be open for business from 8am to 8pm including weekends. The building was later to become a branch of the Blaina Co-operative Society and when the telephones did eventually arrive, the Co-op was allocated the unique number of Beaufort 2.

192. A travelling wagon, once a regular visitor to the district and belonging to the Church Army is seen parked outside the White Horse public house at number 71 The Rise in 1904 possibly endeavouring to enlighten a few customers of proprietors John and Jane Herbert; this was the year of the great 'Welsh Revival' inspired by South Wales miner Evan Roberts who claimed to have converted 100,000 souls in the principality, with the valley towns receiving particular attention. An evangelical movement founded in 1882 by Wilson and Marie Carlile, the Church Army is still a Christian movement caring in many ways for those in need throughout this country, the Commonwealth and The United States.

193. Another long-standing Beaufort public house is the Beaufort Arms, seen here in about 1960 with the former Barclays Bank in the background. Competition for business on The Rise was quite fierce some fifty years ago, for besides the Beaufort Arms the following pubs were all plying for trade such as The Greyhound, Globe, Rising Sun, Prince of Wales and Finers' Arms. November 1839 saw the great Chartist march on Newport by followers of the movement (otherwise known as Scotch Cattle) from all over Gwent, including a large contingent of antagonized men from Rassau and Beaufort, and the Beaufort Arms was to see a little involvement. Local Chartist leaders David Howell, William David, John Jones and William Williams began gathering their men on the evening of Sunday November 3rd, the plan being to congregate at Risca with those making their way from across the county, resulting in an armed force running into thousands in readiness for the assault on Newport itself, that was to end in some tragic circumstances. The Beaufort detachment made their first port of call outside Carmel Chapel at the end of the Sunday evening service, hoping to persuade the parishioners that it was their duty to join them on what they saw as their quest for human justice regardless of what their religious beliefs were, it was more a matter of conscience. It is not known whether any worshippers actually joined the marchers but the numbers had now reached about sixty men, all with a thirst and deciding to descend on the Beaufort Arms for refreshment before the long trek down the valley. They reached the pub at about 11 o'clock at night and the landlord, who was a resolute anti-Chartist, fled in terror after hearing the crowd chanting outside demanding he open up for business. The angry mob eventually broke down the door and in the process of helping themselves to drink, killed the landlord's dog. The extremes of violent protest of course took place on the Monday morning outside the Westgate Hotel Newport, resulting in 22 deaths and although none were recorded as being residents of Beaufort, Brynmawr and Nantyglo were to lose six in total.

194. Soar Baptist Chapel which was erected on the Rise in 1851 and seen here in about 1951. Like many others, the chapel has since closed through lack of support, the building however although now 150 years old has been preserved, completely renovated and converted into private accommodation.

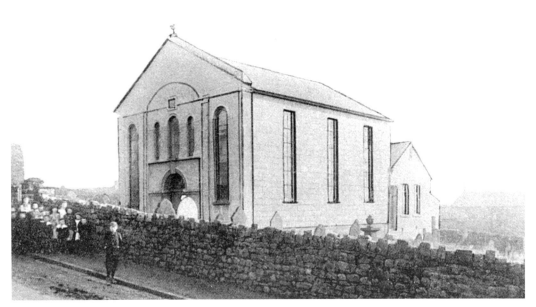

195. Bethesda Chapel, which was on the opposite side of the road to Soar and a little further down the hill was not preserved after closure and was demolished during the 1980s.

196. July 1969 saw the Investiture of the Prince of Wales, with celebrations and local carnivals being organised as usual for such an occasion. These ladies are from the Beaufort and Garnlydan area suitably dressed in national costume for a parade.

197. The celebrated Beaufort Male Voice Choir whose talent has reached a widespread audience particularly with recorded releases and amongst the gathering here are Euan Davies (Conductor), Colwyn Sillman (Soloist), Margaret Davies (Accompanist), Gwyn Evans (Chairman) and many more including Bob Wheeler, Eric Jones, Barrie Mower, Derek Pugh, Byron Watts, Dennis Batten, Josh Williams.

198. An acclaimed 'son' of Beaufort Hill was Thomas Richards who was born in 1859 and left school at the age of 12 to work in the Pwll-y-Garn colliery on the mountainside between Ebbw Vale and Nantyglo. Experiencing miners' conditions first-hand, he dedicated himself to a life-time campaign of improving the miners' lot in South Wales whatever the cost. He formed a small body of local colliers, who saw this as the first sign of any organised unity within the local pits and a voice to be listened to. An unprecedented event, it immediately angered the coal-owners who saw it as a grave threat to their position and he was given a prompt dismissal. This was met with even greater anger by his followers who staged a strike that was to last almost two months before the employers finally agreed to a full reinstatement. From this moment on, Tom Richards' future in industry and politics was duly set. In 1898, he was appointed General Secretary of the newly-formed South Wales Miners Federation and by 1908 saw the movement affiliate itself with the fast-growing Labour Party, thus ensuring a commanding influence throughout the coalfield. Already chairman of Ebbw Vale Urban District Council and a Monmouthshire County Councillor, in 1904 he was persuaded to stand for Parliament in the constituency of West Monmouthshire upon the death of the sitting MP and by now, such was his local charisma, that other challengers were advised it not being worth the time, effort or expense in opposing the candidate; he was duly elected to Westminster with a resounding majority for the time of more than 4,800 votes. In the General Election of 1906 he was elected as the first Member of Parliament for the new seat of Ebbw Vale, one of a total of just 29 Labour MPs throughout the whole of the United Kingdom at the time, a seat he held until 1920 when he made a difficult decision to relinquish his post in order to spend more time with his Mining Federation interests. Unfortunately, less than a year later one of the biggest upheavals in the mining industry ever occurred, with the government returning the South Wales coalfield into private ownership after seizing control in the middle of the First World War in 1916. This led to a bitter conflict, a lock-out and ultimate humiliation for the miners when they had no choice but to save their jobs and return to work after accepting an unprecedented reduction in wages. Amongst Tom Richards' many other interests and achievements, including that of elevation to Privy Councillor, his decision to leave active politics resulted in what was probably his finest hour as far as his mineworker supporters were concerned, eventually leading to his election in 1929 as President of the Miners Federation of Great Britain (the formation of the National Union of Mineworkers not coming into being until 1944). Beaufort's 'Old Tom' as he was affectionately known, passed away in November 1931 at the age of 72.

199. Beaufort Hill Junior and Infants School was built shortly after the introduction of the Education Act in 1870 and designed to accommodate 700 mixed pupils and infants. After closure, the building was derelict for a number of years before fire eventually brought it down in the 1980s, the site having since been built upon. This staff photograph was taken in 1959 and consists of the following, left to right. Back: Jack Wells, Sally Watkins, David Hughes, Dilys Jones, Ivor George and John Probert. Front: Frances Long, Jennie Marshman, Randall Williams (Headmaster), Mavis Lawrence and Mai Jones.

200. Jolly smiling faces of a 'Keep Fit Class' of local ladies suggest that it is not all pain and suffering whilst trying to maintain those curves, the group having been photographed at Carmeltown in October 1969.

201. The Beaufort Welfare AFC Team in 1951 and the players, reading left to right are - Back: G. Williams, E. Hapgood, K. Landman, C. Hayes, T. Walbyoff and R. Hapgood. Front: C. Jenkins, R. Parfitt, K. Edwards, P. Phillips and G. Jennings.

202. Some light refreshment is being taken by members of Beaufort Welfare Rugby Club during a tour to Bournemouth whilst partaking in the Easter Rugby Festival of 1956. A few names to remember are Arnold Biles, Lyn Phillips, Mr. Thomas, Keith Amos, 'Sticky' Powell, Clive Bull and Ken Cameron.

Acknowledgements

The author wishes to express his most sincere thanks to all those residents from the numerous areas covered within these pages for their invaluable help during the compilation of the book. Their contribution, by way of the time spent providing valuable information, the lending of photographs and continual patience has been exceptional. Each and every one has been a joy to meet and learn from and will they all please accept my genuine appreciation of their efforts.

Malcolm Thomas

A further selection of titles associated with the same author.

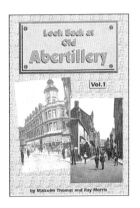

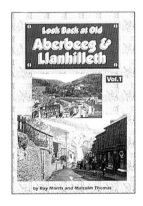

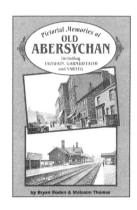

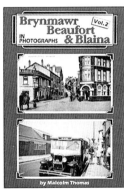